Spencer MacCallum

A Man Beyond His Time

Mike Hamel

Spencer MacCallum: A Man Beyond His Time

Copyright © 2021 by EMT Communications, LLC.

Published by EMT Communications, LLC.

ISBN 978-0-578-87415-9

Cover and interior design by Niddy Griddy Design, Inc.

First printing—March 2021

Contents

Foreword

In writing this foreword to Spencer Heath MacCallum's biography, I struggled to stay on the subject. I was drawn instead to reflecting on my own indebtedness to the person who had the greatest influence on my intellectual life, as well as having been my closest friend of more than sixty years.

Much admiration has been expressed for Spencer's research, innovation, and writing on property-in-land and proprietary administration of communities. His work on these subjects is widely recognized as providing the key to a future for humanity free from the scourge of politics.

I was privileged to witness the evolution of Spencer's revolutionary thinking and writing from its origin in his grandfather's innovations and teachings through his extrapolations and refinements, from the day I met him with his grandfather in 1961 up to his death at the end of 2020. Except for a pioneering sojourn in indigenous Mexican pottery art, for which he was widely acclaimed, Spencer remained at work on community development matters and on preserving the groundbreaking work of his grandfather, from whom he inherited the framework and intellectual direction of his life's work.

My relationship with Spencer was somewhat broader than merely witnessing his achievements. Besides a long, warm, and unwavering friendship and family embrace, I had the benefit of Spencer's insight and encouragement in my work to explain the scientific method and apply it to the development of an authentic natural science of society. Spencer believed my preparation and experience in the physical sciences, a preparation he lacked and for which he felt handicapped, would be instrumental in this crucial development. He was keen to have me develop his grandfather's unpublished ideas on the philosophy and epistemology of natural science, accounting for modern relativity and quantum considerations.

Whether or not my work on the meaning and application of science will ever fulfill Spencer's expectations, there is no doubt that his interest and assistance were significant and productive in this quest. For just as revolutionary as his success in establishing the necessity of adopting proprietorship in place of politics in all social functions is the advancement of a proper natural science of society. He was fond of the expression "Proprietorship is the total alternative to politics," which he coined during his participation in Baldy Harper's Institute for Humane Studies.

Spencer's life was a pageant to behold. It was one unheralded adventure after another of his own making. He led a charmed life and was beloved by many. His enthusiasm for every opportunity to venture was so contagious, yet his remarkable and varied experience was not apparent to those he encountered casually because of his unassuming modesty.

It is regrettable that Spencer did not write his own autobiography. He certainly had the writing ability, storytelling talent, and material to do so. His humility, coupled with other more demanding interests, would not permit it. Fortunately for the rest of society, this timely biography of the man has been skillfully rendered by Mike Hamel.

In this book you will glimpse the life of one who applied his gifts to lofty goals and succeeded far beyond his modest claims. Part 1 chronicles his life as best it can be captured in print. Part 2 lists some of his remarkable intellectual achievements.

Behold a life well lived!

Alvin Lowi Jr.
Chairman of the Science of Society Foundation

Introduction

Ideas are like shadows. They are real, yet they have no physical substance. But unlike shadows, they impact the real world when someone seeks to live them out. Their presence can be felt as they shape religion, science, and society.

This book explores the social and political ideas of Spencer MacCallum and his grandfather Spencer Heath, whose lives spanned from 1876 to 2020. Heath was an engineer, inventor, lawyer, philosopher, and political thinker. His ideas never became popular because he was not an academic, nor did he recruit and train a cadre of disciples. What he did was influence other thinkers, including his grandson.

Although trained as a social anthropologist, Spencer MacCallum didn't pursue an academic career either. He did extensive fieldwork on proprietary communities, helped his grandfather self-publish his works, worked briefly in the business world, ran his own small business, and helped launch an indigenous art movement.

Each man put his main thoughts into print. Heath's magnum opus was *Citadel, Market and Altar* (1957); MacCallum's was *The Art of Community* (1970). In reviewing the latter, urban planner Joseph Gilly writes, "This is without question one of the most thought-provoking books ever published on the subject of alternatives to government as we know it. *The Art of Community* invites us to look to the area of alternatives to political, tax-supported institutions, one of the least surveyed and most promising intellectual and entrepreneurial frontiers of the modern world."[1]

"Alternatives to government as we know it" is one of the big ideas that Heath and MacCallum shared. It promoted proprietary communities as opposed to the state. "It was a breakthrough," notes Alvin Lowi Jr., "because it is precisely that aspect of human life—the quest for community—that provides the traditional excuse for politics and taxation, which inevitably lead away from community toward human bondage."[2] Heath and MacCallum believed private owners could organize and manage communities along proprietary lines and provide public services competitively as a market-based alternative to politically corrupt governments.

Such entrepreneurial communities, or "entrecomms," are privately owned entities that manage real estate, provide services, and create prosperous societies based on mutually beneficial contracts. Proof of concept is evident in proprietary communities such as hotels and shopping centers. "These communities have many competitive advantages," MacCallum said, "including the flexibility of land usage and financial independence. They don't rely on taxation or subsidies. The entrepreneurs who own and manage them have authority to make decisions that are incentivized by the optimal benefit to their communities. Making the communities successful affects their bottom line, the revenues from the land."

One political thinker who has extrapolated what this idea would look like in today's world is Calvin Duke. As he explains in his recent book *Entrepreneurial Communities: An Alternative to the State*:

> I apply MacCallum's framework to much larger communities like cities and modern nation-states. I show how States can be considered contractual communities with grotesquely dysfunctional governance rules that are inferior to entrecomms (entrepreneurial communities) in providing public goods,

just as it is the case of the smaller communities studied by MacCallum. My analysis includes not only the provision of traditional public goods, but other key factors for community health such as the efficiency of managing conflicts, the flexibility in using real estate, and the harmonious selection of community members.

I address how a world without state-sanctioned coercion would naturally evolve into societies based on entrecomms managing land and public services. I focus on those public goods most difficult to imagine as produced outside the traditional State. This includes the definition of laws and the provision of the judiciary and police, as well as what is now called national defense. Along with it, I show how such societies would allow people to flourish, virtually eliminating wars and providing solutions to today's most obstinate problems like massive immigration.[3]

Duke shows in practical detail how MacCallum's ideas can inform and improve everything from private business plans to community development. His work should be emulated by academics, activists, and entrepreneurs because this could help tip the balance in the ongoing struggle between individual liberty and state coercion.

Ideas are seeds that originate in someone's imagination. Once shared, they are either ignored or pollenated by others. They take root and grow into beliefs, practices, and cultures. Good ideas produce good fruit. This book is a brief introduction to a man who has some great ideas that could lead to more humane societies. They deserve to be better understood and applied.

This is the story of an extraordinary individual who almost never worked for anyone else, interacted with and influenced the leading libertarian thinkers of his day, and always followed his idiosyncratic passions. He is also the cocreator of possibly the only viable approach to a stateless world that could actually work.

All of Spencer's words in this book are Spencer's. The vast majority were taken from extensive interviews given at his home in Casas Grandes, Mexico, in 2017 and 2018. Some were taken from published articles. Spencer was not able to participate in the completion of this book, given his unfortunate accident and death.

PART 1
HISTORY

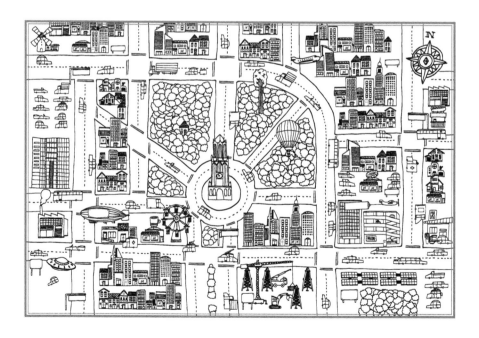

1
Early Years

Spencer Heath MacCallum was born to Ian Crawford MacCallum and Lucile Heath in New York City on December 21, 1931. "My mother told me more than once it was the shortest day and the longest night of the year," Spencer would later say. "When my maternal grandfather, Spencer Heath, visited, he found his daughter crying. When he asked what was the matter, my father answered, 'We can't afford a second baby.' This was during the Depression, very hard times.

"My grandfather left the room and came back in a few minutes with a check for $1,000. That was a small fortune in those days. So, being bought and paid for, I was named after him, Spencer Heath MacCallum. I'm sure this was not the connection, but as it worked out I was the only one in my family who was interested in Popdaddy's ideas. That's what I called him. Much later I would actually work with him. He would sometimes say that $1,000 was the best investment he ever made." (In this book, the elder Spencer will be referred to as "Heath" or "Popdaddy" to avoid confusion.)

"Popdaddy had three daughters and a son who lived only a few weeks," Spencer continued. "In a way I became his son. It was actually better than a father and son because a grandfather and grandson can sometimes have a better relationship. Popdaddy was quite a philosopher. My parents weren't into philosophy or politics. As children, my older brother, Crawford, and I weren't interested in his ideas either and would tune him out. What he said was boring and entirely over our heads. This didn't bother him. He always felt it was up to him to make available to others the best of his thinking but it wasn't up to him to make them accept it. Not until I was at Princeton did I really start to understand some of what he was saying."

Spencer's father, Ian MacCallum, was the youngest of nine children. When he was twelve, he went to work at a steel mill to help finance his sisters' education. The custom in the part of Scotland from which the MacCallums came was to educate the girls so they could marry well. Ian often did his sisters' homework, so he learned along with them. This eventually led to his being admitted to the University of Pennsylvania as an architectural student even though he had not completed high school.

In time, he met and married his wife, Lucy, and started a family. After college he got a job with Warren and Wetmore in New York City, one of the largest architectural firms in the world at the time. He was their youngest architect and one of the last to be let go when the Depression hit.

At the outbreak of World War II, Ian went to London, where his job was to study aerial photos before and after air raids and estimate the damage. He knew and loved European architecture as few people did. The destruction he saw over time changed his psyche.

Back home during the war, Spencer's mother was determined

to expose her two sons to a foreign culture while they were still young. She read in the media about how most trade and cultural relationships had been almost entirely with Europe. After the war, there would undoubtedly be more interest in Latin America. It became her mission to learn more about America's southern neighbors. She decided to move to Mexico, even though she didn't know the language or anything about the culture. She took her nephew Erwin along too.

Lucy planned to stay for the duration of the war, even if it lasted six months. Her visit stretched to almost two and a half years. By then she had three young men with some understanding of Latin language and culture who were better prepared for the postwar world.

"We moved around a lot during those years," Spencer said. "Our pattern was to travel with people we enjoyed being with. When we found a place we liked, we lived there until we met someone else we thought we would enjoy being with and off we went. One time near the end of our stay, we kids thought up a plan for a trip from Mexico City to Mérida in Yucatán by land. Everybody said there's no way to go by land, but we figured out a route. I was twelve, and my brother and my cousin Erwin were fourteen. The three of us wanted to go alone. My mother said: 'Well, if Pedro says it's all right, then you can go.'

"Pedro Armillas was a cartographer and anthropologist who was a refugee from the Spanish Civil War. He had a very level head on his shoulders and knew a lot about Mexico. He was a good friend of the family. My mother never thought he would approve of our plan but he did, so she went along with it. We went down to Veracruz by bus, then took the train across the isthmus to the Pacific. It was quite a trip at night, crossing through the jungle, and we did a very stupid thing. We went to where the cars were connected, climbed down the steps, and swung from one to an-other. After the train we took a bus to a small town whose name I've forgotten. Then we hopped on a little Piper Cub plane that hopscotched across little landing spots in the jungle.

"We made it to the tiny village of Villahermosa. We were to wait for the *Carmen*, a sternwheel paddleboat on the Usumacinta River that had originally been on the Mississippi River. Pedro had told us we must never get separated, but my brother and I fought so much that only one day into the trip we split up. He was a few days behind my cousin and me. We waited for the *Carmen* but it never arrived, so the two of us found a river launch and traveled on it for four or five days. It was a wonderful experience.

"The skipper had a little cabin in the front of the boat that he let us stay in since we were 'extraordinary individuals'— *norteamericanos*. We made it to Tenosique, just a few miles from the Guatemalan border, and we waited for my brother to catch up.

"After a few days Crawford arrived on the *Carmen*. We wanted to see the Mayan ruins at Palenque, but there was no road there, so we backtracked on the *Carmen* to a small village called Emiliano Zapata. We found two trucks headed to a village within walking distance of Palenque and arranged to go on them. They were just bare skeletons held together with who knows what— no glass in the windows, no padding on the seats.

"We made it to the village, and the three of us slept on a long table, sharing a single blanket. In the morning we got to Palenque on horseback, and it was very interesting. Then we traveled another two days on horseback to Tenosique. The only people we saw on that part of the trip were a family of Indians. They fed us beans and coffee and gave us their hammocks to sleep in. During the night we could hear the lions roar from one side of the valley to the other. I remember thinking, *It can't be too dangerous, or these people wouldn't live here.* We learned in the morning that these were howler monkeys that sounded just like lions.

"The next day we almost made it to Tenosique by dusk and had to cross the river to reach the town. There was a broad, smooth path we walked along in bare feet. We would see these big dark things and had no idea what they were. We came to a little house and found a man with a dugout canoe who would take us across the river. When we asked about the things we had seen, he said, 'Oh, those are tarantulas.'

"On the other side of the river we met a group of hunters. They had killed a baby alligator, which they gave to me. They also had an ocelot skin that was still wet from not being cleaned, and I bought that. We took the train from Tenosique to Campeche and from Campeche to Mérida. We had arranged to meet Mother in Mérida on Christmas Eve, but we were a week late. We had sent cables to the hotel where she was supposed to be staying, but none of them reached her. For her part, she had wired every place we were to have been on the trip to find out about us, but she got no replies. Then somehow, we got word to her that we were coming from Campeche, and she met our train. We hadn't bathed on the trip and were filthy dirty. The first thing she did was take us to a public bathhouse to get us cleaned up.

"I think she suffered terribly during our trip, and if I remember correctly, her hair had turned white. She later told me that when she was alone in the hotel, waiting for us, she thought, *What have I done?* Then she said to herself, *Lucy, you can be as scared as you wish, but you must not let that affect what you will or will not let these boys do.* I was impressed with that. She always had a sense of adventure, and she instilled that in us."

After more than two years of this gypsy lifestyle, the

MacCallums returned to the US. Despite having a wonderful sojourn in Mexico, Lucy was unimpressed with the educational system. And she didn't want her teenage boys absorbing the misogynistic tendencies she had observed in the culture.

The time in Mexico had an impact on Spencer. His mother had helped him make contact with some Mexican archaeologists, who sparked his curiosity and imagination. These encounters kindled a fascination with Mexican archaeology, a passion that would influence Spencer's later life. When he was just twelve, he was responsible for discovering a valuable fresco at Teotihuacán.

Spencer developed a severe stuttering problem when the family returned from Mexico to the United States. "I had a lot of pressures on me," he remembered. "I was uncomfortable with my peer group because I'd been away, and I had trouble fitting back in. It was a stressful time, as I was getting prepared to go to Andover for high school."

Additional stress came from Spencer's parents. The war had changed Ian and Lucy, resulting in a long and messy divorce and, for Lucy, suicidal thoughts. But no matter the personal strain, Lucy made sure her boys were cared for. Spencer, now fourteen, went to Andover Academy, the oldest private school in the country. The school, situated in Andover, Massachusetts, had roots that went back to the Revolutionary War, and its fruit included two American presidents and six Medal of Honor recipients. The costly tuition was covered by scholarships, help from Popdaddy, and, as Spencer recalled, "a lot of dishwashing."

Spencer's love of travel and spirit of adventure continued while he was at Andover. One time he went on a summer trip from Canada to Europe. He took his bike and some money and hitchhiked from Massachusetts to the departure city in Canada. But when he couldn't get rides, he decided to take a taxi for a few hundred miles, using almost all his money. He traveled and lived for the next two months in Europe on less than $200.

He arrived in Rotterdam and began cycling south by himself. "I had some good adventures," he said. "I traveled through France to Paris. I could only afford to spend one night a week in youth hostels. The other nights I slept outdoors. Near the hostel in Paris I slept in a cemetery with some others who couldn't afford the hostel. Some of us decided to go to North Africa, and we went around the cafés, singing and playing guitar for donations. I couldn't sing or play, so they gave me a little saucepan to collect the money.

"I didn't end up going to North Africa, but I cycled to Andorra in the Pyrenees Mountains. Riding down into the Loire Valley, I passed English people going very slowly and steadily on their bicycles, but I took my feet off the pedals and just flew. Then I calculated badly going around one curve and was headed toward the edge with a five-hundred-foot drop-off. There was nothing I could do, and I felt myself very removed from it all and wondering what was going to happen.

"Somehow I made the curve, and from then on, no more streaming down the mountains."

2

Proprietary Societies

Spencer followed Crawford to Princeton in 1949. His brother had received the highest score on the entrance exams in Princeton's history up till then. He was a mathematician who went on to study physics, cosmology, and astronomy. Albert Einstein was at the Institute for Advanced Studies at Princeton at the time. "One of my roommates was from Einstein's family," Spencer said. "Einstein was very open to people, and his home was open to students. I regret that I never took advantage of going with my roommate to his home. The extent of my interaction with the great man was saying good morning to each other while crossing a field.

"I couldn't decide on a major," Spencer admitted. "After going through the handbook, I finally settled on art history. I would also minor in biblical literature. The theology department had some art exhibited in their halls that was part of a collection of Northwest Coast Indian art from the late 1800s. At that time it was not considered art at all but simply artifacts. While not particularly valued at Princeton, the collection was known to scholars and anthropologists. (Eventually part of the collection would be exhibited at the 1962 Seattle World's Fair.)

"I was given free rein to study it and dove in. I repainted the exhibit cases and took a lot of photographs. I decided to do my undergraduate thesis on Northwest Coast Indian art. The art department at Princeton had never granted permission for any work outside of the Renaissance and a few other areas, but a professor stood up for me, and I got permission to proceed."

It wasn't until Princeton that Spencer connected more deeply with his grandfather's political and philosophical thinking. Spencer vividly recalled one evening during his sophomore year (1952) when Popdaddy, who loved to drive all over to visit friends, dropped by his dorm room.

"I was feeling very depressed," Spencer said. "I was studying Franz Kafka's *The Trial* for a literature course. Popdaddy was in his seventies then, but still very spirited. We discussed the ideas in the book all night. He helped me see that Kafka was looking for truth. The protagonist kept cutting through layers and webs and not finding it. Finally, he got to the bottom and there was nothing more to cut except his own throat. The conclusion was, if he gave up looking for truth, then he was no longer worthy to live. Popdaddy said, 'Instead of looking exclusively inward and finding a lot of negative emotions, look outside yourself at your surroundings. Then you will begin to see how things really are.'"

From then on, Spencer paid more attention to Popdaddy's ideas. Of particular note was the concept that the only way to understand society was to understand it totally apart from political government. Spencer had never heard anything like this. Over the next two years he listened carefully, asked questions, and raised objections. He knew that Popdaddy was always writing but had never been published. His political ideas were not in favor in the 1940s and 1950s. As he got a handle on Popdaddy's radical concepts, Spencer proposed that after he graduated they could work together to self-publish Popdaddy's book. The title was *The Energy Concept of Population*, which was later changed to *Citadel, Market and Altar*.[4]

"Popdaddy was always on the lookout for conversational opportunities with anyone," Spencer said. "He wanted to share his best thoughts with others but always stopped short of trying to make them accept anything he said. He believed the best thing we could do on this earth is to inspire our fellow human beings.

"One of his big ideas was the concept of society independent of politics. He saw politics as a social pathology. He thought to understand society you needed to look at it in the absence of this pathology to see how it functions in its normal and healthy condition. He had hopes this pathology could be outgrown. He always said, 'Health is more catching than disease. If it weren't, none of us would be here.' When someone would tell him this was a naïve, utopian view, he would reply, 'Was it utopian to expect to navigate the air? A generation earlier, you would have thought it was crazy to do so.'"

When Spencer had exhausted the material in the Princeton library on Northwest Coast Indian art, Popdaddy offered the use of his apartment in Greenwich Village. It was within walking distance of the New York Public Library and two blocks from New York University (NYU). Popdaddy knew of Spencer's stuttering problem and had discovered that the National Hospital for Speech Disorders was nearby. Spencer was motivated to take advantage of their programs. He had met a girl and fallen head over heels in love, and he didn't want his stuttering to be a problem. It had kept him from having much of a social life as a teen. Now he had an incentive and a resource to address it.

"I accepted Popdaddy's offer and left Princeton for a year," Spencer said. "It was a wonderful time having an apartment in the Village just east of Washington Square. It was on the eleventh floor above Rocky's Bar. I went to the National Hospital for Speech Disorders to attend group therapy. I explored the used bookstores on Fourth Avenue and read everything I could find from authors like Sir Henry Sumner Maine. I shared books with Popdaddy I thought he should be reading, and he liked that.

"Every morning I walked to the New York Public Library. They gave me a study carrel, where I kept my typewriter and papers. I would work until they threw me out at night. The next morning I'd go up there again, until I had exhausted everything they had on all aspects of Northwest Coast Indian culture. I recognized early on the connection between their social organization and Popdaddy's ideas about proprietary societies. The Indian culture was clan based and initially stateless."

One of the pluses of staying at Popdaddy's was getting to know some of his friends who had similar political interests. They would become more well known than Heath because they had platforms he didn't, either in academia or in publishing. Many would later credit his influence on them.

There was E. C. Riegel, whom Heath considered to be an economic genius, although he never had much money personally. Riegel was an early consumer advocate in the 1920s and 1930s and subsequently focused his time on studying the nature and function of money before dying of Parkinson's disease in 1955. More on Spencer and Riegel later.

Spencer also got to know Murray N. Rothbard. "He was a very intelligent person with a great sense of humor," Spencer remembered. "He was hospitable and welcoming to visitors. His apartment had books piled from floor to ceiling. I wish I'd taken more advantage of his hospitality while I was staying at Popdaddy's. Murray had agoraphobia, which kept him from flying. It prevented his attending conferences on the West Coast until some psychological treatment helped him overcome it. He eventually went to the University of Nevada in Las Vegas, where he was S. J. Hall Distinguished Professor of Economics until his death in 1995."

David Gordon, Senior Fellow at the Mises Institute, credits Rothbard with "major contributions to economics, history, political philosophy, and legal theory. . . . He combined Austrian economics with a fervent commitment to individual liberty."[5] Rothbard was, a key figure in the American libertarian movement. He coined the term "anarcho-capitalism"[6] and was considered by his peers to be the "conscience" of the assorted breeds of libertarian anarchism.[7]

Another friend of Heath's with whom Spencer became acquainted was Charley Reese. Reese was a reporter and speechwriter who became a syndicated columnist known for his conservative views. He called himself "almost, but not quite, a libertarian."[8] "Popdaddy and Reese had a mutual respect for each other," Spencer noted. "I remember Popdaddy would walk a few blocks to a brownstone where Reese was giving talks to hear his thoughts."

Then there was Russell Kirk, a historian and social critic whose 1953 book *The Conservative Mind* greatly influenced the postwar conservative movement in America. "Popdaddy was always trying to teach Russell about proprietary communities," Spencer said. "He thought proprietary land management would fit in very nicely with what he called a 'dynamic conservatism.'

Russell was very cordial when he later entertained us at his home in Michigan."

Spencer returned to Princeton the night before final exams. He had skipped a half semester of his third year and had to get his professors to agree that he had not been wasting his time and to give him passing marks, which they did. Spencer wound up graduating a year late, though, with the class of 1955. After Princeton, he spent another year with Popdaddy in New York and at his country place in Elkridge, Maryland.

While still at Princeton, Spencer had invited Popdaddy to hear a visiting lecturer, Edward McCrady, vice chancellor of the University of the South in Sewanee, Tennessee. It was an Episcopal liberal arts college and seminary. The two men got to know each other, and McCrady urged Heath to spend the 1956 academic year at the university as his guest.

Heath, now eighty years old, audited advanced theology classes and refined his vision of the Christian doctrine of man. He later presented his doctrine in a series of talks he was asked to give at Chapman College in 1961 by college president and friend John L. Davis. Davis sponsored the lectures and encouraged their publication. This turned out to be the last time Heath spoke in public. The talks were taped, and Spencer would edit and include them in a book he published in 2018, *Economics and the Spiritual Life of Free Men: Re-Imagining Our Emergent World Society.*[9]

Now seems a good place to interrupt Spencer's narrative with a bit more about the man who so profoundly shaped his life and thinking.

3
Popdaddy, aka Spencer Heath

Born in Vienna, Virginia, in 1876 to a well-to-do family of Quaker stock, Spencer Heath had a lifelong love of machines and an intuitive mechanical sense of how they worked. As a child he once took apart his mother's brand-new sewing machine and barely got it reassembled before she got back from town. Another time he built a waterwheel on the stream that went through their property. No surprise he wound up studying electrical and mechanical engineering at the Corcoran Scientific School in Washington, DC.

After graduating he went to Chicago and worked as an engineer for various companies. At age twenty-two he married Johanna Maria Holm, a suffragist and friend of Susan B. Anthony. The Heaths moved to Washington, DC, where Johanna had a job as an admiral's secretary. Spencer found work with the Department of the Navy. Realizing he needed a better income to support a family—eventually he and Johanna would have three daughters—he thought about switching careers to either law or medicine. He concluded that law would probably pay better, so he went to National University Law School at night and earned his LLB (bachelor of laws) and LLM (master of laws) degrees.

Spencer went into practice as a patent lawyer. Personally, he didn't believe in patents, but he saw the need to protect inventors from having someone else steal their ideas. His clients included Christopher and Simon Lake, inventors of the even-keel-submerging submarine. He helped them present their design to the US government, but Uncle Sam wasn't interested. Next they shopped the idea around Europe and found some interest in Germany. No deals were struck, however. But a few years later, during the First World War, the Germans would wreak havoc with their even-keel-submerging submarines.

Another prominent client of Heath's was Emile Berliner, inventor of the telephone receiver and the flat-disc phonograph record. In 1907 Berliner commissioned Heath to design and build a set of rotary blades to test the helicopter principle—that rotary blades could lift the weight of an engine. The test was successful and piqued Heath's interest in the aerodynamics of airplane propellers. He began carving them by hand. Demand was slow at first but grew steadily. One of his best customers was the king of Siam, who had a keen interest in heavier-than-air flight.

By 1912 propellers had become such a successful business that Heath gave up his law practice and moved to Baltimore, where he started the American Propeller and Manufacturing Company and, later, Paragon Engineers. Always the engineer, Heath soon came up with a mechanical process to mass-produce propellers. As a result, his company was in a position to supply about 75 percent of the propellers used by the Allies in World War I.

After the war, Heath's propellers were on the Navy NC planes that made the first transatlantic flight. In 1922 he demonstrated the first successful engine powered and controlled by a variable and reversible pitch propeller. This would be a key to larger-scale commercial aviation. As his business grew, he bought land and a home he called Roadsend Gardens in Elkridge, Maryland, south of Baltimore.

In the late summer of 1929—fortuitously, just a few months before the stock market crash—he sold his aeronautical patents and technical facilities to Bendix Aviation Corporation. After consulting with the company for two years, he retired at the age of fifty-six to Roadsend Gardens. He set up a commercial nursery and devoted himself to experimental horticulture and his longtime interest, a philosophy of science that could lead to a natural science of society. On the engineering front, he continued to publish articles and would go on to be listed in *The International Who's Who* for his contributions to aeronautics.

Heath's friend Fred E. Foldvary described him as "an arresting figure—tall, bald, and white-bearded in a day when beards were scarcely ever seen. The singularity of his appearance was further emphasized by a pince-nez held in place by two black cords tied at the back of his head. He spoke in beautifully constructed sentences, but in a voice so quiet that hearing him oftentimes required an effort."[10]

Spencer detailed how "this began an intensely creative period for Popdaddy. He set out to discover what the successful sciences, meaning those which have given rise to dependable technologies, have in common that could help in the development of an authentic natural science of society. He outlined such a science in his book *The Energy Concept of Population* and called it *socionomy*, reviving a little-used term that *Webster's New*

International Dictionary defined as 'the theory or formulation of the organic laws exemplified in the organization and development of society.'

"Popdaddy defined society in an interesting way. It was that fraction of a population involved in reciprocal services through the market system. Defining society like this makes you realize it is a very recent phenomenon—a few centuries, perhaps—and it is evolving. In this short time it has given us an abundance of all of our basic needs, such as food, clothing, and shelter, that were very difficult to get before. What it has yet to provide is an abundance of public or community services.

"The administration of communities has not changed since earlier times," Spencer continued. "Everything has been revolutionized in our lives except how we conduct our communities and cities, which is through taxation. Popdaddy thought about how we could provide community services contractually and competitively through the marketplace the way we manage everything else. One way was through what we do with land."

Earlier in life, Heath had been attracted to the thinking of nineteenth-century political economist Henry George. Heath had gotten involved with the Georgist movement in 1898 when he became recording secretary for the Chicago Single Tax Club. In 1932 he helped Oscar Geiger start the Henry George School of Social Science in New York City. He taught at the school for three years and gave seminars on community and social organizations.

By 1933, Heath had come to believe that George's ideas about land were wrong and that land ownership was essential to a healthy society. He felt people were fully capable of providing for every social need through the free development of private property. This was the key to outgrowing subservience to the state.

Geiger's untimely death in 1934 at age sixty-one had resulted in Frank Chodorov becoming the school's director. Chodorov belonged to a group of libertarians known as the Old Right. They opposed both the New Deal and the American entry into World War II. Heath's differences with Georgist thinking led to Chodorov dismissing him from the school's faculty. Joseph Gilly describes the breakup:

> Spencer Heath, originally influenced by Henry George and the Single Tax on land, broke with this view over the issue of taxation. He reasoned that public services were a function of land ownership and therefore properly provided by the land owner. Rent is thus the appropriate means of compensating the entrepreneur. Taxation and political administration are replaced by management for profit, with its accompanying efficiencies, reduction of costs, and consequent increase in the standard of living.[11]

"Chodorov did not appreciate that my grandfather was straying from the strict line of Henry George," Spencer recalled. "That's why he fired Popdaddy. (Chodorov himself was dismissed from the school in 1942 because of his anti-war views.) Popdaddy always said Chodorov had every right to fire him if he felt he was 'corrupting the youth.' They remained on good terms, however, and wrote letters back and forth. Popdaddy could never convince him to change his views about land and property. One time, Chodorov wrote him a short letter that said, 'I refuse to get pulled into a Georgist argument, but I'll give you some advice free of charge. Do something else.'"

Heath's friend John Chamberlain was an economic historian, journalist, and a founding editor of the *Freeman* magazine. In

1936 he urged Heath to self-publish his views in a monograph, *Politics versus Proprietorship*.[12] It was the first statement of the proprietary community principle. Another friend, Alvin Lowi Jr., would later write that in this monograph:

> [Heath] showed how proprietary administration is a viable alternative to political administration of that part of community life that is enjoyed in common. This was the breakthrough discovery that had eluded Henry George. It was a breakthrough because it is precisely that aspect of human life—the quest for community—that provides the traditional excuse for politics and taxation, which inevitably lead away from community toward human bondage.
>
> It was a remarkable finding by Heath that communities have owners—i.e. the owners of the underlying realty—who, once they understood their own interest, could organize and manage community enterprises along proprietary lines and deliver public services competitively for profit.[13]

Heath believed taxation was theft, which was a break from traditional conservatism. "He often used the example of slavery in the ancient world," Spencer explained. "Virtually no writers of antiquity, although they may have urged that people treat their slaves and other livestock kindly, ever proposed the abolition of slavery. Slavery was accepted as the basic economy upon which society was established. It was not something that made any sense to question. It was not until technology had developed to the point where people could entertain alternatives to slavery that they could recognize it as an atrocity. The same applies to taxation. Only when people can entertain in their minds alternatives to taxation will they be able to recognize it as theft."

Henry George's landmark book *Progress and Poverty: An Inquiry into the Cause of Industrial Depressions and of Increase of Want with Increase of Wealth: The Remedy* was published in 1879. In the 1890s it would sell more copies than any other book in the US except the Bible. Heath published his critique of the book in 1952, sixteen years after *Politics versus Proprietorship*. The twenty-three-page pamphlet was called *Progress and Poverty Reviewed and Its Fallacies Exposed*. C. Lowell Harriss, former president of the National Tax Association and leading US tax expert, would later write that some of Heath's critiques were worth examining:

> An example of those deserving of respectful attention is the call to look at government's taxation and unwise spending; some of the unpleasant results that George and his followers attribute to landowners' demands for increasing rents (which absorb growing output) come really from the "take" of government. In challenging George's methodology, Heath notes that although George, in opening the discussion that proceeds for hundreds of pages, asserts a determination "to take nothing for granted," the conclusions set forth in *Progress and Poverty* had been reached long before it was written.
>
> An erstwhile Georgist, Heath retained the idea that all public services should be paid for out of ground rent, but advocated that instead of being supplied by government they be supplied by landowners (individually and in association), holding that the market would attract renters to those locations with the best services—including defense. These proposals for social reorganization are developed in his *Citadel, Market and Altar: Emerging Society, Outline of Socionomy*.[14]

The book Harriss mentions, *Citadel, Market and Altar*,[15]

had been completed in draft form in 1946, but it wouldn't be published until 1957. It was Heath's magnum opus. "This book explains, as no one had done before, the functional role of private property in land as the fundamental social institution," Spencer said. "It makes possible the protected place upon which the market depends. It has the potential to provide all manner of public community services contractually in the market."

Reviewing the book for the Free Nation Foundation, Roy Halliday wrote:

> The bulk of this book consists of arguments for private property, voluntary associations, contracts, and free markets. It is hard-core libertarian—even anarcho-capitalist. Spencer Heath's main practical purpose is to encourage landlords to provide services to their tenants in place of state-provided services—so that the state will become obsolete. The most important service that landlords should unite to provide is protection from coercion, in particular they should provide protection from crime and taxation—protection from both anarchy and statism.[16]

The book was published by the Science of Society Foundation, which grandfather and grandson had started in 1956. The foundation was "an educational and research organization dedicated to a wider and deeper understanding of the voluntary institutions of all mankind. . . . The foundation advocates total freedom of the individual based on the sanctity of private property, that is, every human being has a natural right to own, use, exchange, and give away the fruits of his labor without being coerced by anyone as long as he doesn't coerce others."[17]

One purpose of the foundation was to present and promote

Heath's ideas, ideas that had influenced many other political thinkers of his time. He is largely unknown as a social philosopher and political thinker because he was never on faculty anywhere or had classrooms of students to carry on his work.

"When we were together, we talked a lot," Spencer said. "I recorded as much of our conversations as I could. He didn't think much of it was worth preserving, but I did. I was determined to understand what he was saying. He had had successful careers in engineering, manufacturing, and law, as well as being a horticulturist, social theorist, philosopher, and poet. He was a practical man, sensible in all his dealings and very wise. A mission of my life has been to make an archive of his writings so they will not be lost."

Those writings include his seminal pamphlets:

- *Politics versus Proprietorship: A Fragmentary Study of Social and Economic Phenomena with Particular Reference to the Public Administrative Functions Belonging to Proprietorship as a Creative Social Agency* (1936);
- *Private Property in Land Explained: Some New Light on the Social Order and Its Mode of Operation* (1939);
- *Progress and Poverty Reviewed and Its Fallacies Exposed*, updated with supplementary material (1952); and
- *The Inspiration of Beauty, Human Emergence into the Divine by Creative Artistry* (1960).

An overview of Heath's mature philosophy is given by Spencer and Alvin Lowi Jr. in *A Summary of the Philosophy of Spencer Heath*:

Spencer Heath seriously addressed three broad fields of inquiry and showed them to be interlocking: (1) the philosophy of natural science and the nature of knowing, (2) human social organization, and (3) the spiritual life. By spiritual he meant the aesthetic and creative—the non-necessitous part of life, the part that is pursued for its sake alone. Out of these three threads of diverse character he wove a whole-cloth philosophy, a single, unified perspective on human life. . . .

Heath perfected his unique view of the historical Jesus as an intuitive poet who anticipated a world without politics, a voluntaryist world in the perhaps distant future which is only now, two thousand years later, beginning to come about and which he called, poetically, the kingdom of God on earth. That was the vision. But he also had the method, the means, and the social technology to realize the kingdom. The method was the golden rule. It is significant that his rule is stated in the positive form because, when practiced, mutually and reciprocally, it is the sole ethic in capitalist, free-enterprise behavior. It is a command to engage in contracts: to go into business, doing for others in the manner we would have others do for us, which is to say, with regard for their wishes.[18]

Near the end of his life, Heath lived in Virginia near his daughter Lucy. "He was in a nursing home and suffering from dementia," Spencer said. "Occasionally he would have clear days and he would play the piano and entertain the other residents. To the end he was known for inspiring people in one way or another."

After Heath died in 1963, Spencer collected his extant writings and every scrap of paper he could find in the New York apartment and Maryland home. Years later, while living in California, Spencer would begin transcribing pages by hand. Decades later he would use scanners to digitize the roughly three thousand items for the Spencer Heath Archives. It will be housed at Guatemala's Universidad Francisco Marroquín, where Spencer has been a visiting professor.

4
Entrecomms

After graduating from Princeton with a degree in art history, MacCallum spent another year with Popdaddy in New York City and Roadsend. Then he went to graduate school in anthropology at the University of Washington in Seattle, where he would be closer to Northwest Coast Indian life and culture.

"Because these people had a traditionally stateless society, echoing Popdaddy's ideas and those of Henry Maine on the village community," Spencer said, "my interest turned strongly toward social anthropology. I chose to do my master's thesis on Popdaddy's notion of a proprietary, nonpolitical community, for which he often took the hotel as a heuristic model. That's why I went to UC Berkeley in the summer and immersed myself in reading about hotels and how they worked from the bottom up.

"The hotel has its private areas (rooms), its streets (corridors), even a town square (lobby). It has a transportation system that happens to operate vertically instead of horizontally. In all respects it is community but with faster turnover than we are accustomed to. Hotels are entirely contractual, competitive, and market based."

"The principle on which the hotel is organized is that of contract," Joseph Gilly notes, "and the sum of the contracts in effect at any given time might be regarded as the effective charter or constitution of the community. . . . The hotel is proof that contracts can operate at the community level to provide services enjoyed in common."[19]

"This community has owners who provide public services," Spencer added. "To the degree they make the environment attractive to people, they receive revenue in the form of rents. Now, in a traditional community, the ownership is broken up according to who owns the various pieces of land. These owners are not organized the way the owners of hotels are. But can a community function like a hotel? Yes. In many conventional communities we're now seeing more multi-tenant income properties of various kinds.

"I discovered that shopping centers were also a prime example of this since they operate as communities of landlord and tenants. I started reading everything in the library about them. I no sooner approached the end of that research than I realized many industrial and medical parks, office buildings, and marinas were also leasehold communities. Multi-tenant income properties were a widespread phenomenon, but no one had ever studied them as different examples of one thing; what I came to call entrepreneurial communities, entrecomms for short.

"These communities have many competitive advantages, including the flexibility of land usage and financial independence. They don't rely on taxation or subsidies. The entrepreneurs who own and manage them have authority to make decisions that are incentivized by the optimal benefit to their communities. Making the communities successful affects their bottom line, the revenues from the land."

Spencer stayed at Berkeley all winter doing research. Sometimes he would ride his little Vespa to Menlo Park to visit F. A. "Baldy" and Marguerite Harper. He had gotten to know Baldy, a former economics professor at Cornell University, when Popdaddy took him on visits to the Foundation for Economic Education (FEE), which Baldy had helped Leonard E. Read start in 1946. It was among the first modern libertarian institutions of its kind in the country. Baldy was the first staff member, serving as chief economist and theoretician until 1958, when he left to become co-director of the William Volker Fund. In the early 1960s, he was also a visiting professor of moral philosophy at Wabash College.

Shortly after FEE began, Baldy met Murray Rothbard, who would become a key figure in the American libertarian movement. Years later Rothbard would write:

I had the privilege of meeting Baldy in the winter of 1946–47, and from that first meeting he became my dear friend and mentor in the libertarian movement. And I was scarcely an isolated example. For years before and ever since, Baldy Harper carried on an enormous and inspiring correspondence, seeking out all promising libertarians, encouraging any signs of their productivity, by his wise teaching and example developing a large and devoted following of friends and students. . . . In those early days at FEE, almost every staff member had been brought into the movement by Baldy: W. M. Curtiss, Paul Poirot, Ivan Bierly, Ellis Lamborn, all students of Baldy at Cornell. Baldy was indeed a notable inspiration and

guide for young people, and his followers are now everywhere
in the libertarian world.[20]

It's not surprising, then, that Baldy also became a mentor for
Spencer, who fondly recalled, "He was an unassuming teacher
with such a down-to-earth grasp of economics and impeccable
intellectual hospitality who encouraged me to a better
appreciation of Austrian economics and Friedrich Hayek. Baldy
had a great sense of optimism about the future. He adopted
the concept of a 'total alternative' to political government—a
phrase of mine that he and several others adopted. This became
his ideal goal by which to correct and guide mundane decisions
much as the North Star enables the mariner to make continuous
course corrections. The mariner doesn't expect to reach the
star, but steering by it—a process of small decisions and course
corrections—he eventually reaches his destination. Baldy
believed we needed a transcendent ideal to guide our everyday
decisions and keep us on the path heading toward freedom.

"Baldy said he didn't know exactly how he had arrived at
his philosophical position," Spencer recalled, "but he thought
it might have come about from John Chamberlain having
forwarded to him a working draft of Popdaddy's *Citadel, Market
and Altar*. Baldy read it several times and later found himself
advocating a society totally free of structures of institutionalized
coercion. Chamberlain would include Popdaddy's views on rent
in his own book, *The Roots of Capitalism*."[21]

When he returned to the University of Washington in the
spring, Spencer's advisors had trouble with his approach to
multi-income properties in contemporary real estate. They
made him rewrite his thesis, which he did over the summer. "I
didn't have to change that much to get it approved," Spencer

said. "It was good that my undergraduate thesis from Princeton had received the unheard of grade of a perfect score +1. It would have been +2, but I turned it in two days late so they marked it down to a +1. That thesis would later become my book, *The Art of Community*.[22]

"I was intensely enjoying academia at this time. I was engrossed in the study of the evolution of society. I'd go to sleep at night and wake up ahead of where I'd been when I went to bed. It was extraordinary. I thought, *Things are going so well that I could do anything*. So, I went to the University of New Mexico, where my brother was, to take some math courses since I had done poorly in the subject at Andover. I also took some organic chemistry and other subjects. Then I returned to the University of Washington and graduated in 1961 with a master's of arts in social anthropology."

All throughout Spencer's college and graduate school years, Heath continued to introduce him to political thinkers. Sometimes he took his grandson along to the home of Frances Norton Manning in Santa Ana, California. "She invited us out and arranged for us to meet some people she thought would be interested in Popdaddy's ideas," Spencer said. "He was never very good at this kind of socializing, but she was a master at collecting significant and influential people. We met the likes of R. C. Hoiles, of the *Orange County Register*; Walter Knott, of Knott's Berry Farm; John L. Davis, president of Chapman College; [and] Andrew J. Galambos, Donald H. Allen, and Alvin Lowi Jr., the three of whom had worked in the defense industry.

"My relationship with Alvin in particular grew and blossomed through the years. He helped stretch my intellectual grasp well beyond where it was with Popdaddy and Baldy. In particular, I gained an appreciation of the meaning and implications of the scientific method. He became well acquainted with Popdaddy in the time before Popdaddy died. Afterward, he greatly assisted me in organizing and evaluating the Spencer Heath Archives."

Heath had always told Spencer that the people who would catch on to his ideas first would most likely be Jews and engineers. Alvin was both. He had engineering degrees from the Georgia Institute of Technology and a PhD in engineering from UCLA. He served in the Navy as an engineering officer and went on to work in the aerospace industry. Along the way he developed several technologies that he patented. He started his own business that focused on environmentally friendly ways of using energy. Later, Spencer would work on such a project with him in Los Angeles.

"Popdaddy and Alvin talked about engineering, aviation, and physics," Spencer remembered. "Alvin gradually picked up on Popdaddy's consuming interest in the philosophy of science. Using the scientific method as a way to understand society was one of Popdaddy's important ideas. As an engineer, he was very interested in how to apply the scientific method, with its emphasis on experiment, to social organization. It was unfortunate that Popdaddy became ill and had to return home just when they were building such key relationships."

Alvin knew Galambos and Allen from the aerospace industry. In 1960, Galambos left the field and began teaching at Whittier College. That same year he and Alvin met with Leonard Read of the FEE. With Alvin's encouragement, Galambos started his own teaching and research school the following year. It was called the Free Enterprise Institute (FEI),[23] and Alvin became a senior lecturer.

"I met Spencer Heath in 1961 at a Free Enterprise Institute conference promoting Andrew Galambos' course on 'Capitalism, the Road to Survival,'" Alvin recalled. "Heath was impressed to see a crowd attracted to a positive program for cultivating laissez-faire capitalism in the midst of the anti-communist frenzy of the Cold War. Heath was joined by his grandson Spencer MacCallum, fresh out of graduate study at the University of Washington.

"Heath soon became a celebrity in the Free Enterprise Institute community as a result of Galambos' endorsement of his book *Citadel, Market and Altar*, which presented his novel 'proprietary community' proposal. This proposal became a central feature of Galambos' exposition of what becomes of government in a free society not burdened by taxation. Galambos invited Heath to give a course on proprietary communities, but he was well into his eighties, with failing health. Three years later, MacCallum was able to take his grandfather's place as a lecturer. Although suffering from a bad stutter, Spencer succeeded in presenting Heath's thesis to a large and enthusiastic group."[24]

Galambos originally believed in limited government but wound up preaching a stateless society. He was appalled at the state's terrible track record in protecting life and property and likened it to the mafia or drug cartels. This drew its fair share of criticism from those who saw the state as essential for peace and prosperity.

"FEI educated and influenced thousands of people concerning the science of society," Spencer said. "But I didn't learn that much from them because of what I had already learned from Popdaddy. But one thing I did get from Galambos was the various ways that insurance can figure into the successful operation of a free society. He had picked this up from Peter B. Bos, who attended some of his courses. Bos realized that insurance companies had the greatest interest in the safety of property and that they were a critical part of protecting it, and society."

Bos and Spencer became good friends, and Bos would go on

to write *The Road to Freedom and the Demise of Nation States*, which included one of Spencer's articles.

> This book describes why the politically democratic state is a mythical and illegitimate concept that does not and cannot work and why, without the corrective market feedback of profits and losses, this unstable, unmanageable, inefficient and authoritative social organization will cause its own demise. *The Road to Freedom and the Demise of Nation States* maps out an alternative path leading to a new contractual social organization based upon individual sovereignty and freedom.[25]

"I don't think Galambos ever acknowledged the ideas he got from Bos," Spencer pointed out, "but they became an important part of his teaching. Galambos was a genius, but he was also an unpleasant person in many ways. He had this concept he called the 'Moral Island,' and he could kick people off it if they disagreed with him. He kicked about everybody who was closest to him off the island at some point."

In 1961, the same year the Free Enterprise Institute was launched, Baldy Harper founded the Institute for Humane Studies (IHS). He served as its secretary and treasurer until becoming president in 1965. The institute was devoted to "research and education with the conviction that a greater understanding of human affairs and freedom would foster peace, prosperity, and social harmony."[26]

Heath had worked closely with Baldy on planning the institute and even offered him Roadsend Gardens for the campus. Baldy and his family visited Roadsend and enjoyed the place. But in the end he concluded it was too close to Washington, DC, and its more conservative way of thinking. He believed California would be a more hospitable intellectual climate, and in true California style, he started IHS in his garage. IHS stayed in Menlo Park until 1985, when, ironically, it affiliated with George Mason University and moved to Fairfax, Virginia, a DC suburb.

Baldy was interested in breakthrough ideas about society and social organization. He wanted to create an environment that would cater to young people and seasoned scholars. The vital ingredient in his formula would be the give-and-take between the two groups, which could lead to the insights that were sorely needed in contemporary thinking about society.

This approach had worked well at FEE, as Spencer recalled. "People came from all over to their big old Victorian mansion. FEE offered scholarships and internships for young people to stay at the institute and rub elbows with the scholars-in-residence. The dinners I remember were always lively times of discussion that lasted for hours. Unfortunately for IHS, it never developed into all that Popdaddy and Baldy envisioned. Baldy had to spend so much time fundraising. It was painful to see someone with so much capacity and ability having to do this. The ultimate tragedy came in 1973 with Baldy's untimely death."

5
Transitions

Soon after completing his master's degree in 1961, Spencer went to the University of Chicago to start work on a doctorate. Unaccountably, however, his work slowed down. "While continuing to get high marks in my classes," Spencer said, "I often took months to complete course assignments, and my independent work suffered. Finally, after fulfilling the residence and course requirements and everything short of my dissertation, I dropped out.

"I remember one January day when things were getting difficult with my studies. I was lying on the couch in my room. I saw a large kiwi bird with brilliant iridescent colors and a long beak just a few inches from my nose. I understood that if it touched my nose, it meant death. Everything seemed suddenly simplified. I had a solution, a way out of the whole mess—suicide. I thought rather rationally that maybe I should get a second opinion, so I called the hospital and talked to a psychiatrist. He gave me his number and said to call him anytime, day or night.

Things got easier as time went on, and by June the thought of suicide was pretty much gone. I know the bird was imaginary, but I can still see it clearly in my mind even today."

For his dissertation, Spencer had planned to do an ethnography of a shopping mall as a leasehold community of landlord and merchant tenants. The university had given him a summer grant to drive the length and breadth of California, visiting shopping centers and collecting case histories of dispute situations and how they were resolved. This had given him a store of empirical data, and he had even selected the mall in which to do his fieldwork.

"That was not to be, however," Spencer painfully recalled. "I just couldn't do it. My last accomplishment before leaving Chicago was publishing a paper that I still think is important, "The Social Nature of Ownership."[27] For the summer of 1965, I had been invited to consult on a project with the UCLA Economics Department with Armen Alchian and Harold Demsetz. I had difficulty fulfilling that commission.

"I struggled for what I called 'the lost decade,'" Spencer said. "Then it occurred to me toward the end of that time that I hadn't had a physical in quite a while. I went to a doctor, and he determined my problem was hyperglycemia. The condition wasn't well understood back when I was in Chicago. He told me I could cure about 80 percent of my problems simply by cutting out all sugar from my diet. I did it, and my life pretty much came back together, but I never returned to academia."

Some interesting projects did unfold during the lost decade. "E. C. Riegel had died in 1955," Spencer said. "I kept in touch with his family and friends. I thought his papers might contain valuable ideas. That's how, ten years later, I was on hand to save his work from being dumpstered. Riegel had given his material to a friend by the name of Major Firth. They went to his widow when he died, and I offered her $500 for everything of Riegel's she could find.

"Almost ten more years would go by until I showed one of Riegel's essays to Harry Browne in 1975. In his best-selling book *You Can Profit from a Monetary Crisis,* he called it 'the best explanation of the free market I've seen.' A flurry of requests for the essay encouraged me to go through Riegel's material in detail. I was excited to find some of his work had been annotated by Popdaddy. I eventually self-published two books from Riegel's papers: *The New Approach to Freedom* (1976),[28] and, *Flight from Inflation: The Monetary Alternative* (1978)."[29]

In the late '60s Spencer was helping his friend Alvin Lowi Jr. with an ambitious water desalination project near Los Angeles. Alvin had worked on desalination while in the Navy. As a civilian, he developed a process to supply clean water to Los Angeles but ran afoul of utility regulations and couldn't proceed. Spencer described his company, Terraqua Ltd., as "a libertarian venture specializing in water treatment technology and energy management oriented toward community utility systems."

"Spencer gave Terraqua its name, vision, and business purpose," Alvin later recalled. "The purpose was to apply our unique distillation technology to community development.[30] What really intrigued Spencer was the favorable economics of integrated on-site utilities that could potentially free community enterprises and community entrepreneurs from zoning, planning, and licensing hurdles presented by conventional utilities.

"Spencer initially got involved with Terraqua as an investor," Alvin continued. "He had inherited his grandfather's estate plus a large trust account. He sold Roadsend Gardens in Maryland to invest in Terraqua and other projects. He dissolved the trust and used some of the cash to speculate in the Zurich silver futures market, which was being promoted by a hard-money pro-capitalist friend. He ran out of money trying to cover his margins when the silver boom went bust in 1970. His friend left the country."

Spencer became friends with the engineers on the project and enjoyed helping in any way he could. When the company ran into financial difficulties finding working capital and faced bankruptcy because of the shenanigans of some investors who were trying to ruin the company's credit, the engineers, who were also stockholders, didn't want to see the company fail. Not having the time or skills to focus on the business side of things, they asked Spencer to become CEO. Spencer's head wasn't working very well at this time due to his hyperglycemia, but he spent the next six months doing everything he could to save the company, to no avail.

"Some investors had hired a manager who deliberately tried to destroy the company," Spencer said. "One thing he did was remove the quality control at the end of the production line, which led to all kinds of problems with customers. Apparently, his idea was that the company would go under and be put on the auction block; then the doctors could buy all the assets for next to nothing. It was a pretty disappointing situation, especially since the distillation technology was sound and worked well. It could have provided Los Angeles with ultra-pure water at a low cost."

Around this time, Spencer saw an ad from Werner Stiefel, head of the multinational pharmaceuticals firm Stiefel Laboratories. Werner was looking for "libertarian engineers" who knew about floating breakwaters. Spencer didn't know about floating breakwaters, but he wrote to see if Werner might be interested in Lowi's desalination process. Werner wrote back and offered to meet next time Spencer was in New York.

The two later met at the University Club in New York. Werner shared why he was interested in floating breakwaters. He had been born, raised, and educated in the US, but his family had a soap manufacturing business in Germany. It prospered but had to be abandoned when the Nazis came to power. In 1942, Werner, his brother, and his father started over in the US. They built what would become the largest privately owned dermatological company in the world. Werner Stiefel was president and CEO until his retirement in 2001.

Werner believed America was headed toward the socialism that was spreading in postwar Europe and Asia. To preserve a free capitalist society, he would create a libertarian nation in the Caribbean Sea, beyond the legal jurisdiction of any country. He founded and funded the Atlantis Development Company to buy the land and equipment necessary to build his new country. His base of operations was the Sawyerkill Motel in Saugerties, New York, near one of his plants. He publicized his dream and began collecting a team of eager young libertarians.

"Werner knew desalination would be important for the project," Spencer said, "and I was all for his idea, but I didn't connect it with my work on proprietary communities then. That would happen later. We stayed in touch, and he visited me and Alvin when he was in LA. We became good friends. One day we were having a discussion at the Hobby Knobby Coffee Shop in nearby San Pedro, where I lived. Werner was looking glum, which was unusual. When I asked what was wrong, he told me he'd been trying to figure out what kind of government his new nation could establish that would not go down the same tired route of tyranny that governments always do.

"That's when I made the link with proprietary community administration. I talked a bit about this, and he immediately saw the connection and got excited about the principle. Now it was just a matter of working out the details. But I was bone weary and thought to myself, *Do I want to go through all this again?* It was my undiagnosed hyperglycemia. Still, it was a great opportunity.

"Werner had been influenced by Ayn Rand's *Atlas Shrugged* and would call his new country Atlantis," Spencer added. "It would be modeled after her Galt's Gulch. But Rand was a novelist, and Galt's Gulch was fiction. She hadn't done any thinking about how it would be organized. There were no details about its social structure. That's where my thinking about proprietary communities filled in the gaps. You could say the idea of the proprietary administration of public services that Werner would try to implement got its start at Hobby Knobby.

"I pointed out how the motel Werner had in New York was a community," Spencer went on. "It's divided into private and common areas, and he was providing public services there. But instead of citizens, he had customers. Provision and maintenance of community services was contractual, carried out through ordinary business means. Why not keep this nonpolitical form of community organization and transfer it to the ocean?

"People could own improvements on the land in any way they liked, but the sites would be leased. By opting not to subdivide, he would preserve a concentrated entrepreneurial interest in the development extending indefinitely into the future. The master lease form would be the social software to generate the actual written constitution of the community. As a result of our discussions Werner commissioned me to draft a master lease form for Atlantis in return for a 2 percent equity in the venture."

Spencer drew up the master lease form, but his work with

Lowi kept him from moving to New York and joining the effort. He would later offer this outline of Werner's program: "Around 1970, Werner purchased a motel near the company's main plant in Saugerties, New York, and invited libertarians to come and live there while they worked in the surrounding area and, in their free time, to help plan the Atlantis Project. He conceived of the project in three stages: Atlantis I was the Saugerties Motel, Atlantis II would be a ship at sea, and Atlantis III would be a floating community, or perhaps a community on dredged-up land on some submerged seamount. The ship would play an indispensable role as supply vessel and living quarters in the construction phase of Atlantis III.

"In pursuing his vision of freeports at sea, Werner put into motion in a practical way a plan for a wholly proprietary, nonpolitical public authority. Here was his answer to the question of how to have public administration and yet each and every person be fully empowered over his own person and property. He believed that humankind would outgrow government as we know it today.

Perhaps what is most intriguing and heartening about his formula for an internally consistent, open social software is that it is not conjectural, but is extrapolated from a century and a half of empirical data gleaned from observation of the marketplace."[31]

Spencer watched and cheered as Werner poured years of effort and millions of dollars of his own money into the project. At the same time he was running a company with operations in more than forty countries. He knew how to deal with people and difficult situations. Still, Operation Atlantis met with disaster after disaster and ultimately failed.

"The lease form I worked up in 1971 survived Werner's

project," Spencer recapped. "Over the years it took on a life of its own as a way to form a social organization. The most important application was that made in Somalia by Michael van Notten. The form became for me a prime heuristic aid in thinking through questions of community administration in the absence of taxation or bureaucratic regulation. Several iterations were published as the master lease form for 'Orbis,' a cluster of imaginary settlements in outer space. We used this fictional premise because Werner was concerned that governments not be alerted prematurely to the idea of free settlements on the ocean, now called seasteads."[32]

While all this was going on, the Institute for Humane Studies published Spencer's book *The Art of Community*.[33] "Alvin suggested the title," Spencer said. "'Art' refers to the empirical art of community, which I saw developing in commercial, multi-tenant properties in the same way that empirical arts like Toledo steel, dye-making, and the like had developed in the Middle Ages."

One reviewer wrote:

MacCallum has opened the door to some interesting speculation. Imagine an aggregation of proprietary communities making up an urban complex. Suppose every city in the nation gradually evolved to this pattern? Why not the entire planet? If one is governed by contractual obligations, the sum of which is the constitution of the community in which one happens to be at a given time, then what is the function of even a limited political government?

This is without question one of the most thought-provoking books ever published on the subject of alternatives to government as we know it. *The Art of Community* invites us to look to the area of alternatives to political, tax-supported institutions, one of the least surveyed and most promising intellectual and entrepreneurial frontiers of the modern world.[34]

6
Juan Quezada

In 1976, the death of a friend left Spencer in possession of some equity in a gold mine near Deming, New Mexico. It had been a very rich mining concern years earlier, and the owners decided to redevelop it. "I was going there every two months from San Pedro to help with the project any way I could," Spencer said. "One Saturday, after leaving the mine, I checked out the local yard sales. I have an addiction to yard-saling. At home on Friday evenings, I would look up yard sales in the newspaper, mark the addresses on a map, and plot the best route to cover thirty or more the next morning. I never knew what I was looking for until I found it.

"One Saturday I found a piece of pottery that intrigued me. I bought it for fifteen dollars and sat it on my piano, where I would pass it several times a day for the next year. I called it my 'mentor pot' because it taught me the language of Casas Grandes pottery, the area where it was from. Then, one Saturday in Deming, after I had exhausted the yard sales, I went to a place on the far edge of town called Bob's Swap Shop. I found three medium-sized ceramic pots with red and black geometric designs. They were very similar to my pot at home. When these pots saw me, I like to say, they jumped up on their hind legs and shouted, 'Look at us! We were made by someone who knows who he is!' I immediately bought the pots for eighteen dollars each and found myself churning with excitement. They had such integrity of design. The owner did not know who had made them. He said they had been traded for used clothing by a Mexican man a few months earlier."

On the drive back to San Pedro, Spencer's eyes kept returning to the pots on the seat beside him. He decided it would be an adventure to find their maker. He assumed it was a woman since women so often do pottery in indigenous groups. He got the intuitive feeling whoever it was had the potential to become a world-class artist. And on his next trip to Deming, he ventured into Mexico to search for her.

There was only one road going south, and Spencer stopped at the adjacent villages and showed pictures of the pots. He didn't take the pots themselves lest customs think they were prehistoric and confiscate them. Within two days he was directed to Mata Ortiz, a village about one hundred miles from the US border. There was no graded road into the village; it was just a railroad stop. From the town of Colonia Juárez he followed some tire tracks into the mountains and eventually arrived at Mata Ortiz near the ancient Paquimé (or Casas Grandes) ruins in the Mexican state of Chihuahua.

"I stopped a boy on a burro going into the village and showed him the pictures," Spencer remembered. "He led me to a house and rode on. I knocked on the door. A woman invited me in, and a few minutes later, Juan Quezada came in. I showed him the pictures, and he told me he'd made those pots six months ago. My first reaction was, *Well, that can't be, because you're not a woman.* Juan's reaction was he couldn't believe someone would take pictures of his pots and come looking for him. We were both at an impasse.

"As we talked, Juan said he could do much better work than what I'd seen, but no one could afford to pay him for the time and effort it would take. I told him to make examples of his best work, and I would come back in two months. But when I returned, the pots were exactly like what he'd always been making. He had assumed I was a strange gringo who probably wasn't coming back, so why make the effort? Finally, I said, 'Let's try something different. For six months, I'll give you a stipend per month. Whenever I visit, I won't expect any number of pots; I just want you to experiment. Pursue your art in any direction you choose. But whatever you do make will be mine, if that's agreeable with you.' And he said, *'Seguro que sí'* ('Surely yes')."

Juan Quezada Celado was born in 1940 in Santa Bárbara de Tutuaca, Mexico, the fourth of eleven children. His family moved to Mata Ortiz when Juan was an infant. He grew up there and, while still a teenager, became intrigued by pieces of Paquimé pottery he found while wood-gathering. He worked for years to re-create the style using native clays and pigments and experimenting with various firing techniques. He was in his mid-twenties and working as a railroad laborer when he started selling his pots, some of which made it to the States.

"By the time Juan Quezada and MacCallum met in 1976," writes Kiara Maureen Hughes, "Juan was already earning a living from his pottery making. In fact, at the time of his meeting with MacCallum, Juan was working with his brother Nicolás and his sister Consolación on an order of 250 pots for a store in El Paso."[35]

While Hughes points out that Juan Quezada had already been "discovered" by the time Spencer arrived, his elevation to the next level was due in large part to Spencer's belief and investment in his talent.

"On my next trip, I was anxious to see what I would find," Spencer said. "Juan's work this time was an order of magnitude finer than anything he'd made before. It was as if he had been waiting for this 'golden formula' for his life and was now running with it. I decided to run with it as well. For the next several years, I worked full time promoting Juan. At first I didn't sell anything I was acquiring. The pieces were like children to me. But pretty soon I did sell some. I realized my role was to place pieces in good museums and the best private collections. Collectors would see them and get interested in Juan. I saw my role as an intermediary between him and the art collectors and museums. I worked on the assumption that there's no shortage in the demand for quality art and no shortage of people able and anxious to buy it.

"The first museum I stopped at was the Heard Museum in Phoenix on one of my drives back to California," Spencer continued. "I went to the director's office, set one of Juan's pots on his desk, and stepped back, remembering how his pots had spoken to me in Bob's Swap Shop. I would never have done anything like this had I known more about the art world—but it worked. I let the pieces introduce themselves. That's been the approach I've used ever since. When the director saw the piece, he immediately said, 'Let's organize a show. This is something exciting!'

"The Heard Museum became the first to showcase Juan's work. At the time they had a show titled 'The Greater Southwest of Art, Including North Mexico and the Southwest United States.' The director decided Juan belonged in that show. The staff did a beautiful job pulling everything together to make it work. They were so taken by the story of this self-taught potter. That was in May 1977. Next, the Arizona State Museum in Tucson included Juan in their annual winter show. This was followed by more than a dozen shows in major museums over the next few years. In all I spent seven and a half years working full time on this project."

Three years into their partnership, Spencer and Juan were going on a traveling exhibition funded by the National Endowment for the Arts. It would be one of Juan's first demonstrations in the US. As they were preparing to leave from Deming, Bill Miles, a friend and head of the ceramics department at the University of New Mexico, drove over to congratulate them and see them off. Spencer recalled Bill, a professor of art, looking at the pots they were taking. "He said something I've never forgotten: 'I don't know of any artist working in any medium anywhere in the world in any age who has advanced his art as far as Juan has in a comparable period of time. And it's the more remarkable for being entirely self-directed.'"

Spencer's exclusive arrangement with Juan ended in the summer of 1979, but they continued to do business, shows, demonstrations, and other events together for several years. "My stipendiary arrangement with Juan was so successful in its initial purpose of enabling him to advance his art," Spencer said, "that I extended the same arrangement to others, including Juan's youngest sister, Lydia; Nicolás, his brother; and Félix Ortiz."

"[Lydia's] technically precise painting caught the attention of MacCallum," Hughes writes, "who began purchasing from Lydia soon after he established his stipendiary relationship with Juan in 1976. As a result, Lydia's *ollas* were sold alongside Juan's in galleries and museum stores throughout the United States. Due to her close association with Juan and through MacCallum's strategic promotion of the potters and their art, Lydia's work quickly attained recognition within a growing market for Mata Ortiz pottery."[36]

Another local potter with whom Spencer became involved around this time was Félix Ortiz. Félix may have been making pottery even before Juan. "I was moved by the quality of Félix's work," Spencer said. "It had a style and vigor all its own."

Working alongside Spencer was his then wife, Anne Copeland. She had a degree in archaeology from Arizona State University and worked in the field from the mid-1970s through the 1980s. Together they curated a very large traveling exhibit for the potters with a number of major museums in the Southwest and California.

For almost eight years, Spencer had been living off his inheritance from Popdaddy. He made the money stretch, but by the early '80s the money was gone and Spencer was $15,000 in debt. He took a job with the Real Estate Research Corporation in Los Angeles. His main project was a feasibility study for a group of Mexican landowners who wanted to do a development in Baja, California.

"I paid off my debt but didn't really enjoy the job," Spencer said. "A friend had a window-washing business with about twenty-five stores on a small route that he wanted to sell. It was in the Fort MacArthur area of San Pedro. He asked me to help him one week, and I thought, *This is a good kind of work. It's clean, and at the end of the day, I feel like I've helped make the world a little better. Plus, I'd rather not work for anybody, and I could do this on my own.* So, I bought the route from him."

This was the mid-1980s and Spencer was in his fifties. "I was a little self-conscious about washing windows," he admitted. "I had a Princeton education, and my mother had hopes that I would at least be a museum curator by now. I was part of Toastmasters at the time, and I gave a talk on what I was feeling one evening. I called it 'Soapy Dollars.' It actually went over very well.

"I decided to build my business and found that I was very good at getting new clients. It was fun, kind of like collecting bottle caps as a kid. I soon had about 150 clients, which was plenty for my one-man operation. I enjoyed the good, fresh work, and that's how I made my living. For years I had intellectually understood the importance of freedom, but I didn't feel it in my heart and sinews. I hadn't internalized the imperative need for freedom until I had some experience with my own business. I owned it and I was working it. I was an entrepreneur."

7

Expanding Influence

Spencer and Anne were divorced, and in 1986 he met Emalie Caley through a woman named Judy, a mutual friend from Sitka, Alaska. She had asked Emalie to deliver a package to Spencer, since Emalie was going to a nursing program at UCLA. They made connections to meet on a Saturday, which was Spencer's day for yard-saling. She went with him, and Spencer would later say he'd found his wife at a yard sale.

Spencer and Emi started dating and enjoyed each other's company. Emi even helped out in the window-washing business when she had time. The two fell in love and decided to get married, officially tying the knot in 1988 at a Quaker meetinghouse in Princeton, New Jersey. They had moved to Waterford, Virginia, earlier that year to help care for Spencer's mother, Lucy, who was in ill health. They had planned to be there six weeks to arrange adequate help for her, but she kept firing the people they hired. Spencer and Emi wound up living there six years. Spencer sold his window-washing business in California and started a similar business in Waterford.

After Lucy MacCallum died in 1994, Spencer sold that business and the couple moved back west. Spencer told Emi it was her turn to pick where they lived. She chose New Mexico. She had taken a job there, but on the drive out she learned her supervisor had quit. There were some other shake-ups too, so she decided not to take the job. Instead, Emi, a nurse practitioner, accepted a contract to work with teenage girls on the Ramah Navajo Indian Reservation near Pine Hill, New Mexico, a town of about a hundred people. Spencer worked on his grandfather's papers while Emi worked on the reservation. They spent about a year and a half there and made lots of friends.

It was friends who got Spencer and Emi to move to Tonopah, Nevada, when Emi's contract expired. They had met Durk Pearson and Sandy Shaw in some classes at the Free Enterprise Institute and stayed in touch. Durk had graduated from MIT with a triple major in physics, biology, and psychology. Sandy had graduated from UCLA with a double major in chemistry and zoology and a minor in mathematics. Together they wrote *Life Extension: A Practical Scientific Approach* (1982), and several subsequent books and articles on health and longevity.

"Durk and Sandy made so much money from their book that they got a tax bill from California for $50,000," Spencer recounted. "So, they said goodbye to California and moved to Nevada. They were total alternative libertarians and wanted to settle somewhere with the least regulation. They called different places and talked to various chambers of commerce. When they called Tonopah, a small town halfway between Las Vegas and Reno, and asked about zoning and regulations, they were told, 'Oh, we don't have anything like that.'

'What about your building codes?'

'No, we don't have those.'

"Durk went through his list and was finally told, 'Look, the only thing we require is that you not store dynamite inside the town.'

"No wonder they moved there."

When Spencer and Emi were moving from New Mexico in 1996, they decided on a detour to visit Durk and Sandy. Emi paid a courtesy call at the community health office in Tonopah. They had been looking for a nurse practitioner for almost a year and offered her a job on the spot. And when the MacCallums drove around town, they saw a house for sale that looked accommodating. They made a lowball offer, which was accepted. It was just around the corner from the trailer once occupied by Howard Hughes.

Tonopah became their home for the next eight years. At one point Spencer took over a rural mail route from a friend who was leaving. He drove the 230 miles three days a week. The route was so remote he could drive and read at the same time.

The MacCallums other libertarian friends included Richard Hammer, who founded the Free Nation Foundation in 1993. Hammer set forth his radical idea in a pamphlet called *Toward a Free Nation*: "We who want liberty should build our own nation," he proposed. "This idea will stun some, and make others laugh. But it seems possible to me. We have the resources. On this planet there are enough people who want liberty to populate a nation. And there is enough capital—held by investors who want the benefits of free markets, but who need to be assured of the security of their investment."[37]

"The idea of a free nation was considered wacky at that time," Spencer pointed out. "But Richard thought it deserved to be

taken seriously. He set up this foundation, largely at his own
expense, to promote his beliefs. It took a few years, but people
began to respect the idea. We had some good conversations and
learned from each other."

Spencer had set up and funded his own foundation, the
Heather Foundation, originally based in Tonopah. Its goal was
"furthering understanding of society as an evolving natural
phenomenon of spontaneously patterned cooperation among
freely acting individuals." The foundation administered the
literary estate trusts of Spencer Heath, Arthur C. Holden, and
E. C. Riegel. It was also their print publisher, as well as Peter B.
Bos's, Erik Don Franzen's, and Alvin Lowi Jr.'s.[38]

Spencer also knew Kenneth R. Gregg Jr. "Ken was a leader in
the Society for Libertarian Life (SLL)," Spencer said. "It was an
early libertarian student organization started in 1973 at California
State University, Fullerton (CSUF). He was a libertarian historian
who really knew what he was talking about. I could pick up the
phone and ask him a question, and that would set off a whole
discussion of all the ramifications and implications involved.
Ken was a great admirer of my granddad and the proprietary
community. He understood it as well as anybody in the world.
He knew all about the Georgist movement and thought of doing
a book on it, but that never happened."

A book that did happen, and for which Spencer was asked
to contribute a chapter, was *The Half-Life of Policy Rationales:
How New Technology Affects Old Policy Issues*,[39] edited by Fred E.
Foldvary and Daniel B. Klein. Klein was a professor of economics
at George Mason University and the chief editor of *Econ Journal
Watch*. "I met Daniel years ago on one of my visits to IHS
[Institute for Humane Studies]," Spencer remembered. "Much
later, he told me, 'I was a student there, and you were the only

one who paid any attention to me.' We became good friends. He once invited me to speak about proprietary communities at a college whose name skips me. That led to doing a chapter about such communities for his book."

Others noted and appreciated what Spencer was saying and writing. "Spencer MacCallum's work on proprietary communities extends [Spencer] Heath's reality-based approach," observed Bruce Canter, General Counsel at Law at MicroVention, Inc. "In addition to having the benefit of his grandfather's tutelage over the years, MacCallum was uniquely positioned to carry on and further develop his work. As an anthropologist he was able to elaborate on Heath's ideas with the benefit of a richer and deeper understanding of real social and cultural phenomena."[40]

Before this, Spencer had been invited to the 1997 Liberty Fund Conference on the Voluntary City. "It helped settle me once again into thinking and writing on social organization," Spencer said. "The fruit of that conference has been a dozen journal articles, most notably, 'The Enterprise of Community: Market Competition, Land, and Environment.'"[41]

Another writing project would come from Spencer's relationship with Michael van Notten, a Dutch lawyer who cofounded the Libertarian Center in Holland in 1975. Van Notten later directed the libertarian policy research organization Institutum Europaeum. In the 1990s, he got interested in helping Somalia develop a stateless society. Spencer heard about van Notten's efforts and tried to get in touch. The two didn't connect until van Notten, who was coming to Las Vegas to get married, realized Spencer lived in Nevada. He asked Spencer and Emi to help with his wedding, which they did. Afterward, they were in regular communication about van Notten's work in Somalia.

In 1995, van Notten and his partner, Jim Davidson, had begun

work on a plan for the Awdal Free Port on the Gulf of Aden, south
of Djibouti. They intended to develop a multi-tenant income
property that could become a smaller version of Hong Kong.
In January 2000, they established the Awdal Roads Company
in Mauritius, to build a toll road from the free port into the
highlands of Awdal and the rest of Ethiopia.

"Michael had married into the Samaron clan (another name
for the Gadabursi clan) and lived his last dozen years with his
adopted kinsmen in northern Somali," Spencer explained.
"During that time he devoted himself to economic development,
the study of Somali customary law, and clan politics. He was
gathering ethnographic material for a book. He died prematurely
in 2002 and in his will asked me to organize and edit his notes for
publication, which I did. This resulted in *The Law of the Somalis*.[42]

"The Samaron are a traditionally stateless people," Spencer
said. "Many would like full participation in the modern world if
they could do so without coming under the thumb of a political
government. Their idea of how to do this was to lease a portion
of their territory with access to the sea for a private consortium
to be developed and managed as a purely commercial multi-
tenant property. If successful, the Samaron would then have a
thriving free port from which to pick and choose among the
opportunities it would offer for jobs, education, entrepreneurial
ventures, and so forth. It would be their bridge to the rest of the
world. My contribution to van Notten's work came in the form
of the Orbis master lease that I had developed for Werner Stiefel
wherein the lease is a mechanism for creating a proprietary
community. For this I received one hundred shares in the Awdal
Roads Company.

"The project ran into local opposition, and Jim continued
to work on creating business opportunities in Awdal after

Michael's death. I asked Jim recently what were the possibilities of pursuing the project, and he said, 'It could be done, but you would need an entrepreneur who would learn the language and marry into a clan. In other words, it would take another Michael.'"

8
Return to Mexico

Spencer had inherited his mother's house after she died. Its sale enabled him to return his focus to Juan and Mata Ortiz. Although their formal relationship ended in 1979, Spencer and Juan had stayed in touch and frequently collaborated on projects. In fact, 1981 and 1982 were the years of greatest activity, featuring trips to the East Coast, exhibitions, gallery sales, lectures, and demonstrations.

Spencer continued to champion the pottery of Juan Quezada and other Mata Ortiz artists. In a 1994 article in the *Journal of Southwestern Anthropology and History*, he maintained that

the potters of Mata Ortiz, a village on the Palanganas River in Chihuahua, Mexico, have created not merely a cottage crafts industry but an authentic new art movement with an uncommonly high degree of artistic integrity. The originator of this movement, Juan Quezada, was inspired as a youth by painted pottery sherds from the prehistoric Casas Grandes

Indian culture. Guided only by the sherds but with single-minded dedication, he independently invented a ceramic technology, internalized an ancient aesthetic, and taught his fellow-villagers. Over the past 20 years, hundreds of villagers have followed in his footsteps and become potters. Assisted by the author and numerous other outsiders attracted by their artistic and technical accomplishments and their openness to experimentation, the potters of Mata Ortiz are securing a place in the international art world.[43]

Another perspective on Mata Ortiz is offered by Kiara Maureen Hughes in her 2009 thesis, "The Women Potters of Mata Ortiz: Growing Empowerment through Artistic Work."[44] It largely parallels Spencer's account: "I am in agreement with both Spencer MacCallum (MacCallum 1979:52–61) and Bill Gilbert about the importance of Juan Quezada's role in determining the direction that has led to a community aesthetic based on 'individual experimentation and innovations, and away from rigid adherence to tradition.'"[45]

In 1999, Juan invited Spencer and Emi to accompany him to Mexico City, along with about thirty of his family and friends. He had rented a bus for the trip. He was going to meet with President Ernesto Zedillo to receive the *Premio Nacional de los Artes*, the highest honor Mexico gives a living artist. Juan, who was painfully shy and preferred being alone in the mountains, spoke eloquently in front of the president and the TV cameras. When Spencer complimented him on his public speaking, Juan said, "I learned it from you."

In 2015 it would be Spencer's turn to be recognized. He received the Ohtli medal, Mexico's highest cultural award.

He had written many articles on Mata Ortiz, as well as the introduction to the book *Portraits of Clay: Potters of Mata Ortiz.* The story is also told in the Emmy Award–winning documentary *The Renaissance of Mata Ortiz.*[46] By the time the documentary was made in 2010, there were more than 450 potters in Mata Ortiz fueling this phenomenon.

Before Spencer came along, Juan's brother and sister, Nicolás and Consolación, were helping him fill large commissioned orders. "It was Spencer MacCallum who suggested the potters begin to sign their names on the pots," notes Hughes. "Until this point in 1977, the family's production was collaborative. Once they started signing, each began to focus on his or her own production and work independently."[47]

Spencer admitted, "When this all began, I had the idea of one individual who potentially was a world-level artist. I had no inkling that it would come to involve an entire village and affect the economy of a region. So, when I look around now at what's happened, it's affecting the art of northern Mexico. I can't believe I had a role in it."

"Spencer felt secure in what he had done in the little village," wrote Walter Parks, a longtime friend, in his book *The Miracle of Mata Ortiz.* "In a sense he had fulfilled the destiny his mother had prepared him for many years ago. A prosperous Mata Ortiz is his monument."[48]

In correspondence with the author, Parks also recounted Spencer's laid-back approach to his sometimes-demanding lifestyle. He told how in 1986, Spencer rode with him to Mata Ortiz. Seven hours into the trip, Spencer realized he didn't have his passport. "For me, there was nothing to do but return to California," Parks said, "but not for Spencer. He was able to convince a reluctant Automobile Club manager in Tucson to give him an affidavit to enable him to cross the border. Not bad for one who claims he's not a salesman."[49]

"The story Mata Ortiz is not a pure fairy tale," noted a 2007 article in the *Los Angeles Times*. "There is plenty of tension and competition among artists trying to make their marks within a tradition that draws on ancient models but is essentially one man's invention. Quezada himself has been embroiled in struggles to develop his work and control his market. For many years, he gained more recognition in the United States than at home. But in 1999, he won the Premio Nacional de los Artes, Mexico's highest honor for artists."[50]

This whole renaissance almost never happened. At an art event in the early 2000s, Spencer and Juan met a lady who had three of Juan's earliest pots. She told them the story of finding them at Bob's Swap Shop in Deming in 1976. There were three medium-sized pots and three smaller ones. She bought the small ones. When she told her husband that night how she regretted not buying all six pots, he said, "Let's go get the others in the morning." But when they arrived at Bob's, the pots were gone. Sometimes history swings on tiny hinges.

Casas Grandes in Chihuahua, about twenty miles from Mata Ortiz, became a permanent home to the MacCallums around 2003. Spencer had spent some formative teen years in Mexico, and a large part of his later adult life as well. "I had been involved with Juan and the potters of Mata Ortiz for thirty years by now," Spencer noted. "As we got older, Emi and I realized that if we needed care, it was too expensive in the US. We had so many friends in Chihuahua that we decided to move there and be next to people we could trust and who would help us if we needed it.

And we've had no regrets. The people have been so welcoming and kind to us.

"We wanted to help conserve some of the old aspects of the town that were being lost," Spencer added. "With some of the inheritance money from my mother, we bought and restored five old adobes near the plaza and furnished them with largely local antiques. We wanted to help Casas Grandes become a tourist destination. We also hoped to attract writers and artists to come for extended stays. It looked promising for the first year or so, until the US State Department put the kibosh on it. They designated the area as dangerous, which meant insurance companies wouldn't insure school visits or tour groups. We had to sell two of the houses, but we still have our flagship, *La Casa del Nopal*, the House of the Cactus."

Walter Parks and Richard O'Connor shared fond memories of the MacCallums' hospitality:

Their masterpiece was the Casa del Nopal, a 19th century house, so dilapidated that a large Nopal cactus grew out of the roof. Completely restored and furnished with antiques, it became a place for archaeologists, writers, and tourists to stay. The MacCallums moved to other nearby houses, including their last, Casa Roja. Wherever they lived, their home always was a stopping place for old and new friends, and sometimes even tour groups on their way to Mata Ortiz.[51]

At Casa del Nopal, Spencer and Emi invited their longtime friend from San Pedro, copper lace artist Lieve Jerger, to come live and work on her seventeen-foot sculpture *La Calesa de los Amores Perdidos* (The Carriage of Lost Loves). The carriage grew its four wheels in Casas Grandes. A few years later, Lieve helped fulfill Spencer's dream of publishing Popdaddy's ideas in a book. Lieve put together the first publication of *Economics and the Spiritual Life of Free Men* in 2018.

The town of Casas Grandes, with a population of around five thousand in 2010, has roots that go back to 1661. Its first mission was built in 1663 and destroyed in the Pueblo Indian Revolt of 1680, when the natives drove out the Spanish for a period. The town is near the ruins of Casas Grandes, circa 700 to 1450 CE. Originally known as Paquimé, the Spanish called it Casas Grandes, "Big Houses." It's the most important archaeological site in northern Mexico and one of the largest in North America.

"The city played a key role in the transmission of knowledge and goods between the cultures of the Pre-Columbian desert southwest and those of Mesoamerica," according to the *Ancient History Encyclopedia*. "Although only 20% of the site has been excavated and surveyed, UNESCO designated Casas Grandes as a UNESCO World Heritage Site in 1998 CE."[52] The area is famous for a particular type of ceramic pottery known as *Ramos polychrome*. This is the style that the Mata Ortiz potters studied, emulated, and modernized.

On December 10, 2020, Spencer was hit by a vehicle while at a gas station in Deming, New Mexico. He suffered nine broken ribs, a punctured lung, a broken hip, and two cracked vertebrae. He was airlifted to the ICU at the University Medical Center in El Paso, where he underwent surgery. After recovering he returned to his home in Casas Grandes.

"We're making the most of our lives," Spencer said, "including entertaining friends old and new. I spend time working on Popdaddy's archives, and I continue writing. I hope to inspire in a few others the passion for life that I've come to feel in these later years. My mother said that her seventies were the best decade of her life for sheer, silly fun. I've found the same thing extending into my eighties."

9

A Friend's Eulogy
Spencer MacCallum:
(1931–2020)

Spencer MacCallum died on December 17, 2020, just four days before his eighty-ninth birthday. No more fitting summary of his remarkable life can be penned than that of his friend and mentee, Zach Caceres, which is reproduced in full with permission from the author.

Spencer MacCallum and the World He Made:
A Eulogy (1931–2020)

Spencer Heath MacCallum, born 1931, died today [December 17, 2020] in Casas Grandes, Mexico.

Spencer is the grandson, heir, and namesake to inventor Spencer Heath. It was Spencer MacCallum that carried Heath's ideas and spirit into the 21st century. To understand the remarkable life of Spencer MacCallum, we must first understand his grandfather.

Heath (born 1876) is one of those Victorian-era polymaths that makes you wonder if modern humans have declined.

He was a successful patent attorney, horticulturist, engineer, entrepreneur and, later in life, a political and economic theorist with a large volume of writing.

Heath is perhaps best known as the inventor of a particular type of propeller which gave flight to early aircraft of the WWI and interwar eras.

The story goes that Heath, the grandfather, got into an argument with none other than a young Franklin Delano Roosevelt. FDR then occupied the humble office of Assistant Secretary of the Navy which managed armament procurement—including for the United States' nascent air force.

Heath believed a certain propeller design would fragment at high speeds—a death sentence for pilots. FDR demanded that Heath's company send the propellers anyway. Heath refused. FDR explained, "Mr. Heath, put those propellers on the train tomorrow or I'll have you shot for treason."

What to do? Heath could either risk his life and stand by his principles or send innocent airmen to fiery deaths.

Heath shipped the propellers.

And yet no plane with the defective propellers ever left the ground.

The night before the shipment was loaded on the train, Heath broke into his own factory with an employee and stamped the crates with bold red letters: "CONDEMNED BY MANUFACTURER."

Problem solved.

This moment from Heath's life speaks to a defining principle of Spencer MacCallum's own life: don't fight against problems, transcend them.

"Transcend the problem" sounds like a feel-good platitude.

But to transcend problems does not mean "think positive" or "hope it goes away." Spencer's belief in transcendence is based on his deep understanding of society as evolutionary. Long before disciplines like computing and economics provided the language of "complexity science," Spencer saw society as a complex, evolving system.

Problems exist for a reason—and the reason is often not obvious. Stubborn problems suggest a systemic issue that can't be fixed by tinkering at the edges.

For Spencer, reality is as it is. There's no point in complaining. To solve problems, you don't create things to "fight" the problem. You create new things that draw people and resources that fuel the problem in a different direction. You *starve* the problem. And, if you're lucky, you might just render it obsolete.

Transcending problems was more than armchair philosophy for Spencer. It gave him a rare moral courage and willingness to venture where others wouldn't. And this took him to some unlikely places.

The Ballad of Juan Quezada

Spencer is most widely known for leading an economic and cultural transformation in the Casas Grandes area of Chihuahua, Mexico. This regional renaissance has an unlikely source: handmade pottery and Spencer's totally unreasonable commitment to promoting it.

In 1976 Spencer visited a junk shop on the US-Mexico border. He spotted some beautifully painted clay pots with no manufacturer marks or names. "I knew as soon as I saw the pots," Spencer later recounted, "that whoever made them was someone special, someone who truly knew themselves."

He bought the pots. The junk shop owner knew nothing more than that the pots had been sold by some people from Mexico.

By any reasonable standard, this is where the story should end. Spencer should have gone home, put the pots above his fireplace, and enjoyed his retirement (*yes, his greatest achievement was a retirement project*).

But that's not what happened. Spencer transcended the problem. He drove into Mexico with *no information* to search for the artist who made the pots.

And, even more unreasonably, Spencer actually found him.

The artist's name was Juan Quezada. He was a farmer in the hills of the remote town of Mata Ortiz. This was the 70's: there were no paved roads. People still used donkeys to get around. Quezada could not read and spoke no English. But he was a first-rate craftsman who derived his novel designs from fragments of indigenous pottery that he found in the hills.

Spencer and Juan Quezada became friends and business partners. Spencer became Quezada's patron and paid him to continue to experiment and create new works. Meanwhile, Spencer, an anthropologist by training, traveled the United States to bring notoriety to Quezada's masterpieces.

Today Mata Ortiz pottery is a recognized artistic style. Single pots can fetch enormous sums at auctions and in fine art galleries around the world. Quezada took on apprentices. An industry was born. Apprentices evolved their own unique spins on the style and made names for themselves. The whole story was immortalized by PBS.

A local friend described Spencer's death as "the end of an era for a whole region in Mexico." This is no exaggeration. The surrounding area is full of potters and the pottery industry provides a livelihood to a majority of the town. It's hard to overstate Spencer's positive impact in the Chihuahua region over the past decades.

And it's hard to *understate* just how challenging an endeavor this was. The deserts of Chihuahua are beautiful and full of kind and hospitable people. But, as with so many regions unlucky enough to be in the shadow of the U.S.'s War on Drugs, Chihuahua is no picnic as a place to live and do business.

When I first met Spencer in 2012 he arranged for a local taxi driver to take me safely from Ciudad Juárez to Casas Grandes. After crossing the border from El Paso, Texas, the driver told me to lay down on the floor of the car so no one could see me while we drove through the desolate streets of Juárez at 3AM. I'll never forget the boarded up shops, the stray dogs, the pale streetlights—the chilly emptiness of a city where you don't venture out at night.

Spencer faced endless problems with broken infrastructure, corruption, thievery, and narcotraffickers running wild. Spencer began construction of a factory to make artisan jewelry in the area, hoping to repeat the success with pottery. Unfortunately for him, the factory was seized by *sicarios*—machine-gun toting hitmen. Just like that, hundreds of jobs and opportunities for local people vanished into the dry desert winds.

And yet on he went.

Spencer's way of being belied his enormous courage. He was slight of stature, unassuming, kind. He spoke so softly he was often hard to hear. While no doubt some will think this is a case of waxing poetic after someone's death, I can honestly say I *never once* heard Spencer speak ill of anyone.

Riding around Casas Grandes in Spencer's old pickup truck he pointed to a house on the outskirts of town.

"That's where the local thief lives," his wife Emi said. "He broke into our house and stole some things."

"And what did you do?" I asked, expecting a swashbuckling tale.

"I went over, knocked on his door, and asked him to return what he stole," Spencer said matter of factly. "And he did."

Citadel, Market and Altar

For his work in Mata Ortiz the government of Mexico nominated Spencer for the Order of the Aztec Eagle—the highest honor that Mexico bestows upon foreigners. Without an ounce of bitterness, Spencer told me that his nomination had been withdrawn after the government discovered his writings on the problems of authoritarian state power and the positive and central role for entrepreneurs—rather than politicians—in society.

I believe Spencer MacCallum is one of the most underrated political theorists of the last 50 years. Spencer had no professorship. He was not an academic. His work is not widely read. I had the privilege of awarding him an Honorary Doctorate from Universidad Francisco Marroquín a few years ago. But he never received the intellectual recognition he deserved.

Spencer had a beautifully contrarian take on the modern world. "Rather than being in 'late stage capitalism'—a period of decadence and decay—we are actually in capitalism's infancy."

Spencer hated the term *capitalism*. He thought it put undue focus on a single element in the system: capital. Much more important to Spencer was the social role of entrepreneurs as coordinators of capital, land, and labor.

Entrepreneurship was a magic elixir of civilization, channeling the creative powers of people to serve one another in ever more efficient and useful ways. For Spencer, the modern world resembled a sort of miracle: huge numbers of people voluntarily collaborating on this massive project we call society.

Spencer's worldview was that humanity had only begun to explore the possibilities of entrepreneurship. His inner anthropologist saw the violence, corruption, and oppression of the modern nation state as vestiges of our barbaric past. In a sense, we still live in a world where warring kingdoms have claimed territorial authority and work hard to extract as much value as possible from those who live within the castle walls.

Spencer saw society as composed of three functions: citadel, market, and altar.

The *citadel* represented the necessary functions of courts and policing—the fundamental requirement of civilization being freedom from arbitrary violence. A good citadel enables the *market*: the free and voluntary exchange of goods and ideas between people. The market, to Spencer, is a pro-social institution and profit is the indispensable compass for whether your actions serve the needs of others or not.

But the citadel and the market were mere stepping stones to the *altar*.

The *altar* represents the spiritual aspirations of humankind. By spiritual, Spencer did not mean a specific religion like Christianity. He rather meant something more like the peak of Maslow's hierarchy of needs.

The surplus of a well-functioning *market* and safety provided by the *citadel* provides the only environment where humans can be liberated enough to pursue the beauty of art and other creative, spiritual pursuits. Creativity's central role in the evolution of society made Spencer reject the use of aggression and violence—no matter how lofty the purported goals. You cannot coerce creative achievement and so, for Spencer, violence is the enemy of a civilized society.

Bitcoin, Patents, and the Progressive Power of Competitive Markets

It's worth noting that despite Spencer's affection for markets, he was resolutely *not* a conservative. He transcended "left" and "right."

He and his grandfather were heavily influenced by the progressive social reformer Henry George. George is most famous for his criticism of landlords as exploiters of tenants. Indeed, George's ideas are the basis for the board game *Monopoly*. Both Spencer and his grandfather knew George and studied at his school in New York.

Spencer also rescued the work of progressive monetary theorist and consumer advocate E. C. Riegel. Riegel believed centralized money would eventually be used by states and crony capitalists to rip off the common person. In an early vision of Bitcoin and other cryptocurrencies, Riegel proposed private, competing currencies that could not be easily inflated—since inflation harms the poorest members of society most.

Riegel's widow had thrown her husband's life's work in a dumpster after his death (one wonders what Riegel did to invite this posthumous honor . . .). Spencer literally climbed in the dumpster to rescue the work. And now we know about E. C. Riegel.

Spencer's grandfather, Heath, did not even like the patent system—believing it was a state-mandated monopoly. Heath took out patents defensively so he could not be sued by competitors, but then refused to defend his patents in court.

"I prefer to let my competitors copy my innovations," Heath once said. "They focus on my old ideas and so they're always *following* me."

The Entrepreneurial Community

Spencer's whole philosophy was bound up with *community*, a stark difference from the hyper-individualistic strands of market liberalism on which critics usually focus.

Community is indispensable for humankind. We are nothing without each other—without the massive collaboration that a free society provides. And that's why violence and authoritarian control are so dangerous.

Spencer's writing on community is unique and refreshingly concrete. His most important work is *The Art of Community*, a small, obscure, but shockingly futuristic book published in 1970.

The Art of Community is an anthropological study of primitive forms of what Spencer termed "entrepreneurial community." From the standpoint of 1970, these entrepreneurial communities were trailer parks, hotels, the then-growing world of shopping malls, airports, and—in the jargon of real estate development— other "multi-tenant income properties."

So what exactly do trailer parks have to do with the future of capitalism?

Spencer's argument is that these developments are unique in the economy. Rather than providing a physical product, the entrepreneur-operators of these developments are providing *community*. Entrepreneurial communities are not built *for* entrepreneurs, but built for others *by* entrepreneurs.

Community, for Spencer, is the combination of physical and social elements that define a place. It's also the core product and value proposition of traditional government.

A hotel, for example, has embryonic forms of all the elements that define community. A hotel provides security guards, cameras, fences, and other tools for the safety of residents. There are shared spaces, such as a lobby or gym, and private spaces like a hotel room. The architecture and design try to offer an inviting environment so people can meet with one another for business and personal activities. A hotel even offers a primitive public transportation system—the elevator.

Spencer was aware of the seeming absurdity of this idea: how can you compare an elevator to the New York City subway or a hotel lobby to Times Square? But this is exactly what Spencer's evolutionary worldview would predict: we are in the *early* days of entrepreneurial community.

We wouldn't go back to 1850 and judge a strong horse by the standards of a Lamborghini. It would be a mistake to travel back to 1970, find the nearest mainframe computer, and assume—as so many did—that these clunky behemoths held nothing interesting for the future of mankind.

Pay attention, Spencer was saying, these unimpressive little developments: the trailer park, the mall, the hotel, the airport, they're the seedling forms of something that will grow much bigger.

The key to unraveling Spencer's major idea is to understand the unique nature of land. The landowner that leases land and space to tenants, rather than being the parasite of Henry George's world, is an *entrepreneur of community*.

The value of land rises and falls in accordance with the value of the physical and social elements that the entrepreneur provides. This is why every homeowner wants to live near a new subway line and why the higher floors of an apartment building—better views—are more expensive than lower floors. Community is all about the spillovers. A community entrepreneur can only survive in the market if the physical and social elements that they provide—the community—is worth more than their costs.

The beauty of entrepreneurial community is that these arrangements are voluntary. I can choose a hotel as a traveler, I can choose a mall as a store owner. This drastically reduces the level of abuse and exploitation that can occur. Spencer was not a utopian—he recognized that entrepreneurs given monopoly powers would also exploit residents just as states do. His hope was that a large and competitive market in entrepreneurial communities would grow over time.

Spencer saw the growth of the "enterprise of community," as he eventually called it, as the natural evolution of the market. The entrepreneurial community is the key to unleashing human creativity—disciplined by profit and loss—to the hardest problems that humankind faces: the provision of common services like roads, environmental stewardship, security, and dispute resolution. The future, so Spencer hoped, held a world where these services would be provided in a peaceful and voluntary fashion.

Many years after Spencer wrote this book, I was reading through the archives of the World Economic Processing Zones Association (definitely a beach read, if you're wondering). I was shocked to see Spencer's pattern of entrepreneurial community unfolding through the decades of meeting minutes. The teams in these discussions build shipping ports, airports, free zones, large real estate developments, and even new cities around the world.

The trend was unmistakable.

In the early days of the 70's, these "communities" were little more than empty land, a road, some fences, and maybe a 5-year tax incentive. But over the decades, they became more complex, more holistic—more resembling of real, flesh-and-blood communities.

By the nineties, these teams were arguing about how to best provide their own manufacturing facilities to tenants, housing for workers, and concierge services to more easily incorporate a company or get the right to work.

By the 2000's these teams were proposing autonomous courts—so that residents and businesses could escape corrupt courts in the surrounding country—training and schools for adults and children, childcare, parks, and services that are indistinguishable from those provided by city governments.

I am convinced that Spencer is right about the future. We're in the early days. And the growing pains we see, rather than discourage us, should inspire a new generation of entrepreneurs to build communities. We face a wild and wonderful frontier.

Earlier this year [2020], Spencer was run over by a truck in New Mexico. The thought of Spencer being crushed by—pardon me—some reckless moron behind the wheel is too painful to bear. As seems to have been his habit, Spencer showed remarkable resiliency over 2020. But, in the end, it was too much. Though cancer couldn't claim him—the injuries he suffered at the hands of an inattentive driver did.

RIP Spencer MacCallum: cherished friend and mentor; a man imbued with the creative spirit of humankind; a man beyond his time; a man who remade the world for the better. You will be missed.[53]

PART 2
WRITINGS

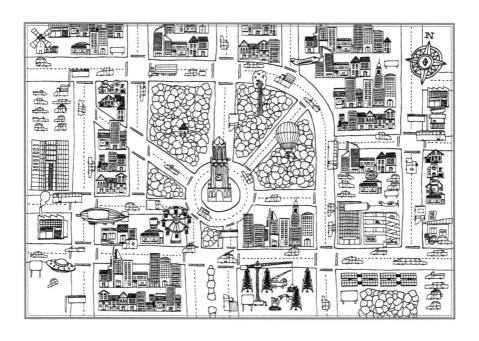

Spencer MacCallum wrote many books and articles and gave numerous lectures over the years. Most of these can be found online, and I've provided links at the end of this book. I have selected four articles for part 2 to give the reader an overview of Spencer's political ideas in his own words. They are presented in chronological order, with text and footnotes as they originally appeared.

"In Search of a Word: Limited Government versus 'Anarchy,'" (1996)

"The Quickening of Social Evolution: Perspectives on Proprietary (Entrepreneurial) Communities" (1997)

"The Enterprise of Community: Social and Environmental Implications of Administering Land as Productive Capital" (2003, rev. 2007)

"Freedom's Ugly Duckling: A Fresh Take on Private Property in Land" (2015)

10

"In Search of a Word: Limited Government versus 'Anarchy'" (1996)

Bumper Hornberger once remarked in a letter to me that in early life he had called himself an "anarchist" but that now he endorsed the concept of "limited government." He indicated he'd had many discussions leading to his change of mind, discussions that had pretty thoroughly covered the field, he felt, and now he wanted to put his attention elsewhere. I was puzzled but didn't pursue it, as Bumper hadn't invited me to and, in any case, I had no wish to divert his attention from the demands of the Future of Freedom Foundation, which he and Richard Ebeling were just getting well launched.

What Bumper's discussions covered I may never know, but the value of holding the ideal of a "total alternative" to political government, as Baldy Harper, founder of the Institute for Humane Studies at George Mason University, once put it to me, seems so profound, as well as wholly unobjectionable, that I feel not so much an obligation as an aesthetic resolve to marshal some thoughts on the matter.

As prelude to the discussion, however, let me put forth one fact that doesn't enter into the argument but that is not irrelevant, either. Many people are now of the opinion that it has been demonstrated both practically and theoretically that taxation, however commonly indulged in, is unnecessary at the local community level. This lack of any compelling need for taxation was shown practically by the experience of the two English "Garden Cities," Letchworth and Welwyn, and by developments in real-estate in this country, which I documented in *The Art of Community* (Institute for Humane Studies 1970). As to theory, the proposition has been exhaustively analyzed by economist Fred Foldvary in his *Public Goods and Private Communities: The Market Provision of Social Services* (Edward Elgar 1994). This raises an interesting question. If it doesn't offend either experience or reason to contemplate altogether voluntary alternatives to the present political administration of community services at the local level, are such alternatives not conceivable at *all* levels of society? For those who are inclined to say categorically no, the challenge for them is to identify where the line shall be drawn. If on some scale private alternatives are both possible and practical, *at what scale* do they cease being so, and why? The prospect of mankind outgrowing government *as we know it*, i.e. financed by non-market means, can no longer be dismissed as pure fantasy.

To elaborate just a little further: if proprietary administration of common services works in a regional mall, which is a real community of landlord and merchant tenants representing a kaleidoscopic play of differing interests and views, then it might work as well on a somewhat larger scale, as in a "new town," which can be a complex of residential, commercial and industrial uses. In fact, we find that it does, as in the British cities of Letchworth and Welwyn and as approximated in Disney World in Florida. And if it works now on the scale of neighborhood and town, might it not ultimately work on a broader scale through towns and proprietary regional associations cooperating? In principle, is there any point on a graduated scale of size that we can point to and say, at this point *proprietary* administration can no longer work; at this point we must embrace *political* administration? Is there any place we can draw a line and reasonably defend our decision?

The plain fact is that we do not know and cannot know what the future holds. But from what is already known, we cannot reasonably rule out the possibility that social evolution will continue and that entrepreneurial provision of our common services will evolve *even as free-market means of feeding, clothing, sheltering and getting ourselves about have evolved in the last 300 years.*

With that background, let's now come to the question of *limited government* versus *anarchy* and which term, if either, a thinking person could adopt as his philosophical badge. (And so as not to let it cloud our minds, let's try to leave out of account the fact that anarchy, as popularly understood, is a pejorative term, bringing to mind images of terrorism.) Baldy Harper, Leonard Read's first associate at FEE and later founder of the Institute for Humane Studies, looked at it in a way that I find attractive. He had no more idea than the man in the moon whether we or our descendants will ever actually see a "total alternative," as he put it, to political, tax-supported-government. But he pointed out the importance of holding the *ideal* clearly in mind as a heuristic device and a compass to help us keep moving always *in the direction of freedom.* The analogy he used was that of the north star and the mariner who steers by it. The mariner doesn't expect to reach the star. But, steering by it, which is a process entailing innumerable small decisions and self-corrections, not one of which he could make without the star, he eventually reaches

Liverpool. We need a transcendent ideal always in mind, Baldy would say, to help guide our everyday decisions that determine whether or not we keep on our heading toward freedom.

That's why I'm less than fully satisfied with the ideal of "limited government." Whether mankind will ever regain the completely free society we know he enjoyed at the pre-state level, where the authority of the village headman was the same *in kind* i.e. authority over his person and property and not that of anyone else, as that exercised by the poorest member of the village, it will probably not be for you or me to know. But while we live, *let perfect liberty be our guiding star.*

The "limited government" concept cannot serve reliably as a guiding star because it is relative; *any* government at virtually *any* time or place in the world is limited with respect to some other government, real or imagined, that might be named. So we must ask, limited by comparison with what? The same criticism is often leveled at the label "conservative." Conserving what? Neither of those two could serve as a north star to keep us to a true heading toward a totally voluntary society, which heading may or may not be asymptotic. So Baldy Harper was an idealist, for the most practical of reasons.

My grandfather, Spencer Heath (1876–1963), a close friend of Baldy Harper, was likewise a practical man. He had not one but a series of successful careers, engineering, law, manufacturing (his plants in Baltimore turned out more than three-quarters of the propellers used by the Allies in World War I), and horticulture. Finally, at age 55, he retired to his country place outside of Baltimore and for the next 30 years devoted himself entirely to philosophy, primarily with reference to science and society. I am currently collecting and organizing his papers for publication on CD-ROM. In the course of this work recently, I came across the following paragraphs which bear on the point of this discussion.

Every thoughtful individual entertains ideals of goodness, truth and beauty, absolutes towards which he can move and aspire but which his own limitations forbid him ever fully to attain. And these conceptual absolutes are no less valuable for their being only relatively and never absolutely attainable. They afford no final goals, but they do establish the directions in which the affairs of men can lead them into endless yet never perfect realizations of their hopes and dreams.

It is the same with the institutions of men. Unless they are ideally conceived as moving towards absolute and hence unattainable goals, there is no ideal guidance, no certain direction, for limited yet ever-expanding achievement towards absolute ideals. This power of conceiving ideals, this subjective conceptual capacity that knows no limitations or bounds, this power of conceiving the Absolute as God, is what distinguishes the spiritual, the creative, from the merely animal, the unregenerate man. This unlimited power to dream, this inspiration of the Divine is the key to man's creative power.

Elsewhere he was even more pointed:

Practical considerations forbid that we should look on these (or any) ideal conceptions as goals or end conditions completely attainable in themselves. Their vast value lies not in their attainment but in their orientation of our energies consistently in the *direction* of these ultimate ideals.

Bumper, are you listening? If so, help me find a better word than "anarchist" (it repels me as being sterile and negative) or a briefer way of stating Baldy Harper's position. Baldy didn't have an all-encompassing word, but he wasn't beating any drums for government, limited or otherwise. He would explain, without any flap about it, that he was drawn to the vision of a "total alternative" and was always on the lookout for breakthroughs in thinking and social technology that might move us in that direction.

Spencer H. MacCallum, "In Search of a Word: Limited Government versus 'Anarchy,'" *Voluntaryist* 82 (October 1996), http://voluntaryist.com/articles/issue-82/search-word-limited-government-versus-anarchy/

11

"The Quickening of Social Evolution: Perspectives on Proprietary (Entrepreneurial) Communities" (1997)

Years ago I read a translation, supposedly true, of a very early Egyptian sequence of hieroglyphs that said in effect that the world was going to the dogs. After listing a number of lamentations, including the disobedience of young people and how they no longer respected their elders, it ended with the observation that "everybody's trying to write a book."

So it always seems to every generation that the world is disintegrating. There's a good reason it should appear that way, a very understandable reason. The world is in flux, with new forms always evolving out of the old. We are familiar with the old patterns because we have lived them, but not with the new, emerging ones, because they have never been part of our experience. Consequently we rarely recognize the new patterns that are in process of forming. Knowing only the patterns that were, all we see in change is disintegration—patterns being lost. This is particularly easy to see in language, in the losing efforts of pedagogues to train the young to speak "grammatically." But the same phenomenon occurs in all areas of our experience. So the disintegration lamented by the early Egyptians and probably every generation before and after is, for the most part, appearance only. It could just as well be called integration rather than disintegration, except that we don't have the evidence before our eyes. We must take it on faith.

The same is true of societal change—the broad sweep of human social evolution. Only evolutionary change isn't gradual but seems to be punctuated by abrupt shifts from one plane of comparatively stable forms to the next—always building on what went before. It's like a stair consisting of treads and risers. The treads are long eras of comparatively stable institutions, whereas the risers are periods of turbulent change and instability that must be negotiated before the next broad tread is reached, just as the spawning salmon must negotiate the steep rapid or rocky waterfall before reaching the next comparatively calm stretch of river. The salmon leaps and falls back, leaps and falls back, but each time it progresses farther and falls back not quite as much, until it negotiates the waterfall.

Mankind has been negotiating a waterfall for at least nine thousand years—an exceedingly brief period in the eons that man has occupied the earth. His leaping and falling back again is the all-too-familiar pattern recounted in history textbooks, the seemingly endless rise and fall of civilizations.

The previous broad tread on the stair, the calm stretch of water we have now pretty much left behind us, was that of tribalism, characterized by dependence on systems of kinship status for sorting out all the customary roles and activities in society. Now relying less on kinship, humankind is experimenting with a wide assortment of contractual relations. Sir Henry Sumner Maine was sound when he observed more than a hundred years ago in his classic study, *Ancient Law*, "We may say that the movement of the progressive societies has hitherto been a movement from status to contract" ([1861] 1986, 141).

I believe we salmon have now reached the point where, as we leap, we can just begin to see over the top of the falls or rapids to the next calm stretch in our river. We can just begin to discern and make some judgments about what the nature of human society will be as it stabilizes once again on the next broad tread of evolution. I'm going to take the risk—I don't think it's a very great one—of making some predictions about human society as it settles into comparatively smooth swimming in the twenty-first century—and probably for quite some time beyond.

Tribalism versus Today's Nation States

Consider first where we've been. As an anthropologist, I've focused a good deal of my attention on tribal societies. In many ways the era of tribalism, as compared with today's world, was a golden age, to be exceeded only by what is yet in store for us. Tribal life, however, left much to be desired. Tribal man's technological proficiency was so limited that he was constantly at the mercy of nature. This limitation was particularly serious with regard to health; general life expectancy of less than thirty years barely permitted biological replacement. A second grave shortcoming under tribalism was that human social life coalesced, as it were, in antagonistic droplets scattered over the globe with little communication or cooperation between members of one and those of another. Opportunities were essentially limited to the circle of face-to-face acquaintances into which one was born.

Notwithstanding such serious drawbacks, tribal society had a positive side. Within each of those antagonistic droplets, social relations had an orderliness and sense of fair play almost incomprehensible to us today. Society consisted of small management units, quite human in scale, and relations among the members (at least among the men) tended strongly to be egalitarian, fair, and just. The headman of a village, for example, though he usually enjoyed more influence and prestige, exercised no authority over the person or property of anyone else in the village. He had the same authority in kind as that exercised by the humblest member. There was no conscription of persons, no taxation. Tribal society was consistent in this respect throughout. Freedom in the juridical sense is this: when one enjoys full integrity of his person and property, he is said to be free. Tribal society was free.

Let me tack a caveat onto that generalization. It doesn't include transitional forms on the boundary between tribes and states. When tribes cross that boundary and become states, they may retain many of their tribal characteristics for a long time. We know we're dealing with a state, however, when force has become institutionalized and is accepted as proper conduct within the group. In *The Art of Community*, I described the example of the Cherokee in 1761 forming themselves into a state (1970, 98–99). The moment of transition was definite, although many tribal characteristics persist to this day. The Cherokee fell within our generalization before 1761, but not after.

Modern society under the rule of political governments presents the reverse image of tribal society. Imagine humankind as a bird attempting to fly. Whereas under tribalism one of its great wings dragged on the ground, preventing it from rising into flight, now that great wing is up and the other drags. In science and technology we've made enormous gains; we've more than doubled our average life expectancy within a few generations and may do so again. We can seek opportunities for fruitful communication and exchange with other human beings virtually anywhere on the earth. That much is progress. But in our political life we have regressed. For example, 268 million people in the United States are ruled monolithically from the top, and their chief executive, a warrior (commander-in-chief of the armed forces), regularly exercises an authority that differs absolutely in kind from that exercised by private citizens in their day-to-day affairs. People have become ciphers, their individuality erased; our gains, even in science and technology, are endangered by the uncontrolled—and apparently uncontrollable—growth and spread of naked force.

The prospect of life under the rule of the nation-state is bleak indeed if seen only from the viewpoint of the disintegration of the institutions and lifeways we grew up with and know from our grandparents' accounts and from reading. But change, as I have noted, characteristically occurs not only from but toward. It has two modes, one quite invisible almost until we bump up against it. Patterns newly forming are not encompassed within our experience; hence we see only the disintegration that change brings. What of the future? Will human society ever get both wings aloft at the same time?

Past experience should reassure us that in the broad picture, at least, change is more integrative than disintegrative. This tendency is demonstrable, for in the long run if health were not more catching than disease—to use a homey phrase of my grandfather's—none of us would be here today. But happily we salmon have reached a point, almost at the top of our rocky waterfall, where we need not rely on philosophic conjecture alone. In our mind's eye, at least, we can begin to see over the top of the falls, and with that glimpse of the future we can begin to recognize and relate events happening all around us. We can begin to perceive fundamental evolutionary changes taking place in the structure and function of our social organization, changes so imminent that I predict we will soon bump against them.

The Change That Is Gathering Speed

How can such change be happening? Let's review some basics. Certainly one of the most significant differences between tribalism and modern society is man's vastly greater facility with numbers. The ability to manipulate numbers makes possible on the one hand the whole world of science and its applications and, on the other hand, that of commerce—both utterly strange worlds to tribal man. Facility with numbers is not by itself a sufficient cause, but it is prerequisite. Without it there could be no science or commerce; with it, given the right conditions, science and commerce will evolve. Science becomes possible because at bottom it involves comparisons of quantities, and every ratio is a number—hence the rationality of science. Likewise, commerce becomes possible, because it depends on numerical pricing and accountancy of debt, credit, inventory, and trades. Change in pricing coordinates the whole world of economic activity.

Science is not my focus here; it's not the dragging wing. The dragging wing is our interpersonal relations, and a fundamental part of those relations—the healing and growing part—is commerce. Do you remember the passage from the Psalm about how the stone that the builders rejected became the chief cornerstone? Commerce is that cornerstone. We appreciate it far too little, and we depreciate it far too much. Alfred North Whitehead once characterized civilization as the "victory of persuasion over force." He elaborated, saying, "Commerce is the great example of intercourse in the way of persuasion. War, slavery, and government compulsion exemplify the reign of force" ([1933] 1967, 83).

Commerce developed as people learned to balance their accounts numerically, making it possible to do business with strangers—people of another lineage, clan, or village. Without numbers, which make it possible for every transaction to be balanced and complete, something is always left over on one side or the other. When dealing with familiars (the language under tribalism, incidentally, is that of gifting rather than buying and selling), that imbalance doesn't matter; over a lifetime or some similarly extended period of reciprocating it all evens out. With accountancy, however, every transaction can be complete in itself, and the parties can depart satisfied without any expectation of seeing each other again, necessarily. So for the first time we can do business with people we don't know. This capability dissolves the surface tension of the antagonistic droplets of tribal society and makes possible the worldwide system of reciprocal services that today gives us our very comfortable standard of living.

My interest here is not just commerce in any of the usual array of things we find in the market, but specifically commerce in land. We're all familiar with the growth of other kinds of commerce, but commerce in land has lagged behind in its development. One of the reasons for its lagging, perhaps, is that in Europe before the revolutions of the eighteenth century, land wasn't free to any great extent—at least not generally so—to become the object of commerce. It couldn't readily be bought and sold in the marketplace. That situation changed only when the revolutions brought about a separation of land and state. This change is not remarked upon in the history books, but it is arguably one of the most important events of modern times. Until it happened, land in western Europe was not free to be traded as other things were but was tied up in primogeniture and entail and was part of the administration of government. Only when the revolutions that swept through Europe divested the titled nobility of their political power and trappings without divesting them of their land could land become a commodity like other things.

The titled nobility as a class tended not to be entrepreneurial; they had previously been the government, and their ethic militated against their dirtying their hands with trade. (In her recent book, *Systems for Survival* [1992], Jane Jacobs clarifies beautifully why this ethic prevailed.) So commerce in land, a truly businesslike approach to land ownership, got off to a late start, and a slow start at that. Even today the vast majority of landlords carry on their business as a sideline to supplement, say, a pension or other retirement income and have little understanding of the business they are in.

The Business Rationale of Land Ownership

The business rationale of land ownership, as explained by Spencer Heath (1936), derives from the fact that public services— the things that we enjoy in common rather than separately and apart from one another, things such as streets, public safety, and other community amenities—are supplied to sites rather than to individuals, and individuals gain access to them through their occupancy of those sites. Thus owners of land, when they lease or sell sites, are the market purveyors of those public services. Only thus can such services be distributed as other goods and services are, through the conventions of the market place. Only through property in land can they be freely and equitably administered by contract, which is egalitarian in the free tradition of tribalism, instead of through favor and privilege, forced levies, the corrosive status relationship of ruler and ruled by whatever name.

This purely distributive function is the land owner's minimal role in society, for which he is recompensed minimally in either land price or rent. Traditionally landowners have done little more. In the entrepreneurial community, however, they are going beyond that minimal distributive function; here they produce the services they purvey, and their rewards are correspondingly greater.

Ground rents, then, represent the going market value of community services and amenities. But the owners of entrepreneurial communities are more than just passive recipients benefiting speculatively from such land values as may haphazardly arise, however important to society that distributive function may be. These owners are systematically generating land value by employing their land as productive capital.

For a model of how this contractual provision of public services even now is occurring, look at the shopping mall in its internal organization as a community of landlord and merchant tenants. The mall or, for that matter, any of the many kinds of multitenant income property in real estate, is smaller and more specialized than most of the communities we frequent, but it is a community nonetheless. It is divided into private and common areas, and the members have a clear arrangement for providing common security, utilities, planning and maintenance of the common areas, and other functions its continuity requires. Yet all of this provision is accomplished through a complex web of contracts without taxation or legislation. It is spontaneous order, arising out of voluntary relationships among the parties themselves.

The rationale for this spontaneous order is as follows: The

proprietor of that place invests in improving it in ways that create an attractive human environment for people to transact their affairs. To the extent he succeeds, and no more, those finding it attractive will competitively bid up rents among themselves for the privilege of locating there. These rents, in turn, finance the public services in that place. Because such communities yield a revenue, they are self-sustaining; they need never become obsolete, like the ruins of Nineveh and Tyre. Because they produce income, someone is both willing and able to maintain them, to renovate them when necessary and even rebuild them to keep them competitive.

These proprietary communities, so called because they are freely offered in the marketplace by the organized owners of the underlying ground, are newcomers in the evolving world of business. Also called entrepreneurial communities, or "entrecoms," they appear in a thinner slice of recorded history, even, than recorded history represents of the total period of humankind's life on earth. They evolved a bit in the nineteenth century in a rudimentary way, as I've described in *The Art of Community*, but they began to blossom only in the twentieth century. Albeit still small and specialized, these multiple-tenant income properties are appearing as shopping centers; land lease communities of manufactured housing that have metamorphosed from mobile home parks; hotels and motels, some of which today, like the Ambassador City Jomtien in Thailand or Las Vegas' MGM Grand, accommodate more than 10,000 guests; marinas; office and research parks; medical clinics; large residential apartment developments; and combinations of all of these forms. The combinations are particularly significant because they represent departures from special-purpose in the direction of fully generalized communities.

Note that entrecoms include neither condominiums nor their close cousins, subdivisions with homeowners' associations, but consist exclusively of communities in which title to the underlying realty is kept intact and parceling is accomplished by renting or leasing.

The rapidity of this development is astounding. Consider the shopping center. Fifty years ago it was experimental; fewer than a dozen existed in the United States, and even the name had yet to be coined. Today there are over 40,000. Moreover, each now supplies for its tenants a significant portion of the community services formerly provided exclusively by local governments, services such as paving, streets, sewerage, parking, and security.

Theorists of Proprietary Community: Henry George, Ebenezer Howard, Spencer Heath

There is scarcely any theory to explain or support the proliferation of proprietary communities. Such theory as exists was developed over the last century by people outside of academia whose work and writing are little remembered: Henry George, the toast of the world in his day but now largely forgotten, died in 1897; Ebenezer Howard died in 1928; Spencer Heath in 1963.

Henry George, a truly remarkable economist, political scientist, and orator, made a major contribution at the end of the last century. He had distinguished predecessors, including among others William Ogilvie, Thomas Spence, Patrick Edward Dove, and the early Herbert Spencer (see Ogilvie [1782] 1970, Spence [1775] 1920, Dove [1850] 1910, and Spencer [1851] 1969). But none approached the forcefulness with which he publicized the idea that ground rents—revenues from land—constitute a "naturally ordained" fund for financing all public services. Unfortunately, the method he envisioned for applying the principle was for government to collect those rents, leaving the landowners out of the picture. Hence Georgist communities in theory would not have been proprietary nor in any sense competitive or entrepreneurial. His reliance on the coercive powers of government—his "going political"—probably accounts as much as any other single thing for his land argument having fallen into obscurity. Fred Foldvary's recent book, *Public Goods and Private Communities: The Market Provision of Social Services*, has only now, a century after George's death in 1897, begun to reintroduce into academic and public discussion the notion of funding public services with land rents.

Like Henry George, Ebenezer Howard, a practical and unassuming Englishman, was a social dreamer of extraordinary vision. Despite his modest personal means, he founded England's Garden City movement and was responsible for the successful development of two entire cities outside London on what had been rural land. Today Letchworth and Welwyn are prosperous cities financed entirely by ground rents, and to my knowledge not a penny of taxation has ever been levied in either. On the contrary, the British Labor government after it had nationalized both following World War II—a private company owning a town being entirely out of line with the political ideology of the time—was embarrassed by the flow of income it found itself receiving. Not being entrepreneurially inclined, it didn't know what to do with the money. Howard and George didn't see eye to eye personally. But Howard, who steered clear of government, considered his wholly nonpolitical "garden cities" the practical application of the Georgist ideal.

Strangely, Ebenezer Howard's work has fallen even more into eclipse than Henry George's. His principal innovation, financing the community from private land rents and thereby dispensing altogether with local taxation, has been forgotten in the literature of city planning; his book *Garden Cities of Tomorrow* ([1902] 1965) is one of those pedestaled and unread classics.[54] The purely physical innovations of his cities, on the other hand, such as design and density control, functional zoning, and the greenbelt, are remembered and widely imitated. But what Howard himself considered his lasting contribution to civilization is worse than ignored; it is simply forgotten. It was considered too radical, perhaps, to warrant emulation.

Howard was uncommitted as to whether proprietary communities should be entrepreneurial ventures or, alternatively, nonprofit trusts. But to help secure support and backing, especially from the Fabian Socialists, who, including George Bernard Shaw, were among his foremost boosters, he chose the latter form. His accountant, C. B. Purdom, writing in later years, attributed the slowness of the two cities in getting off the ground and the general lack of vision of their subsequent management to the absence of any provision for equity in the ventures (1949, 345). The resulting mediocrity may explain why the two cities have made little history. They have not done much more than provide an attractive and successful living environment for 80,000 people! As one supporter plaintively wrote:

> Howard and his associates made one propagandist mistake in siting Letchworth and Welwyn—building them in England within an hour's journey of London. One should have been built on some remote island like Mauritius, and the other in the Soviet Republic of Uzbekistan. Planners and journalists would then have visited them and written them up, and we should have had lots of illuminating books on them. Also we should be excited about them as wonderful achievements, and

be wanting to know why we can't have new towns of the same type in Dear Old Stick-in-the-Mud England. (Osborne 1946, 36)

Spencer Heath was an engineer, manufacturer, horticulturist, poet, and ultimately philosopher of science and social thinker who did his main work during the years of Roosevelt's New Deal, an age of ascendant government in America. That he was not an academic and was "politically incorrect" may help explain why his social theories gained little hearing. The turning point in his thinking occurred in the early 1930s, when he concluded that proprietorship was nature's alternative to politics. In 1936 he self-published a monograph titled "Politics versus Proprietorship." That and his chief published work, *Citadel, Market and Altar* (1957) are now out of print.

Spencer Heath's genius was to see that Henry George's program, which would remove all taxes from private production and finance public services entirely from ground rents (hence the name "Single Tax"), was profoundly in the landowner's interest. For if private production were freed of all taxes and restrictive regulations, productivity and incomes would soar, sites and resources would come into high demand, and rents would rise more than enough to defray the costs of government, leaving a margin of profit to landowners. He believed enlightened real estate interests ultimately would take the lead in removing taxes from private industry and assuming full responsibility for the costs of government. Heath coined the phrase "proprietary community." He completed Howard's concept by providing it with an entrepreneurial engine. By envisioning landowners assuming all the functions of government as we know it, he anticipated the public business becoming private business, a wholly new field for free-market experimentation and investment.

Foreseeing the Evolved Society

If we paint pictures of the future with a broad-enough brush, we can often cover the entire subject and find ourselves "right on." The more interesting predictions, because more difficult, get into specifics. I'm confident in predicting that proprietary community administration will replace political, and although timing isn't to be construed as part of the prediction, I wouldn't be surprised if it happened within the lifetime of many of us living today. The broad picture I envision—timing aside—is one in which financially self-sustaining communities will have become the norm—entrepreneurial enclaves with leaseholds instead of subdivision lots as the land tenure of choice for commercial and residential uses alike. All taxation and burdensome licensing, regulation, and other restrictions on enterprise will belong to the past. The state will have withered away, to borrow Marx's vivid image, its functions progressively better served in an ever evolving marketplace.

More detailed predictions are apt to carry me onto the shoals. Mindful of the danger, however, I am willing to venture answers to the following frequently asked questions.

1. What will happen to national boundaries?

They will become relics of the past, and this outcome is safely within my broad prediction. Should it prove convenient, boundaries between federations of autonomous communities might arise following natural features such as rivers or mountains or cultural, linguistic or other interfaces.

2. Will the communities be all alike?

The variety will far exceed anything seen today, as communities will specialize to appeal to every taste, each discovering its ecological niche in the overall economy. Entrecoms differ greatly even today. Take as a single example the hotel, and count the number of different types. We find resident, resort, transient, "extra-transient" ("hot-pillow"), ethnic, dormitory, casino, budget, and others, with subcategories and hybrids of them all.

3. How big will these communities be?

Size will be determined by market considerations. Except for highly transient and some other specialized situations, I suspect that, as in tribal society, "optimal size" for administrative purposes won't be larger than the largest feasible "face-to-face" community, that is to say, not more than a few thousand persons, in which the manager can recognize members at sight. At successive levels, such entrecoms will cooperate as chain or franchised businesses do today to accomplish functions more effectively handled at higher levels. Customers' preferences will be the determinant. Some communities will clump up together, resulting in high-density urban aggregations of population, while others will be rural. Inevitably there will be elaborate composites of communities of different types and specialties, smaller ones sublet within the matrix of progressively larger ones—just as different kinds of atoms are mutually attracted to form complex molecules, and those molecules cells, and so forth.

4. Will future society be democratic?

The word *democracy* has two meanings. It can mean individual autonomy where all are equal in their authority over their own persons and property, or it can refer to a political decision-making process in which the outcome is determined by voting. Jonathan Swift is said to have commented on the latter kind of democracy, wryly saying that "some people have no better idea of deciding right from wrong than by counting noses."

Political voting, though its intent—and very often its effect—is to moderate autocracy, nevertheless entails people ganging up against one another and is altogether different from making decisions based on property rights. Rule by a voting majority can be as oppressive to the losers as the most autocratic regime. In a condominium or any other subdivision in which the residents have organized to make decisions through voting and thus have departed from purely proprietary processes, therefore, we find the seed of the state. Subdivisions with owners' associations contrast starkly with entrepreneurial communities, and the two ought never be confused.

The homeowners' association is a policing arrangement organized to enforce the restrictive covenants in the deeds. The entrecom on the other hand seeks to foster an attractive living environment that will draw new patronage and keep its existing patronage. These goals differ greatly, and the psychology varies accordingly. In the one the residents are quite literally subjects; they are subject to the deed restrictions and must be made to comply. In the other they are customers. The owners' association seeks compliance and must be rigid; the entrepreneur seeks patronage, and therefore must be flexible and accommodating.

Although owners' associations are often called democratic, on the grounds that decision making is accomplished through voting, entrecoms are no less democratic, inasmuch as the residents vote each time they pay their ground rent. These usages reflect the two different meanings of the word. Both subdivisions and entrepreneurial communities doubtless will coexist well into the future, and therefore both kinds of democracy. I believe without a doubt, however, that voting democracy will become the exceptional rather than the prevailing form. The reason is not merely that leasehold permits flexible and continuous redevelopment even to the layout of the streets without infringing property rights—a definite advantage in a world of increasing technological change. A more fundamental reason is that leasehold permits the entrepreneurial community to operate for profit whereas the subdivision cannot. This feature affords an important measure of protection against arbitrariness not present in the subdivision arrangement (MacCallum 1996, 18, II. D.6 and footnote 6), and it brings an entrepreneurial dynamic to the provision of public services that is wholly lacking in subdivided communities.

5. What about people who prefer subdivision lots to leaseholds?

The idea of owning their own plot of land presently appeals to many people, and where there is a demand, the market usually finds a way to provide. Some communities doubtless will offer approximations to subdivision through the use of long-term leasing, including perpetual leases, paid-up leases, and life estates. But in any case fee-simple properties will probably be available in most parts of the world for as long as anyone cares to look ahead.

6. Will this be like feudalism?

Not feudalism, but manorialism; the two are often confused. Manorialism is a form of agrarian social organization, whereas feudalism is a military order imposed on manorialism, often by conquest, which then becomes largely fused with it. Norman feudalism was imposed on manorial England after 1066.

If the question is whether entrecoms resemble manorialism, the answer is yes, essentially. But manorialism, though structured as proprietary communities, could not progress because it was before its time.

Sol Tax, a teacher of mine at the University of Chicago, did fieldwork in the highlands of Guatemala and wrote a book called *Penny Capitalism* in which he described a system of Indian markets that was purely laissez-faire in the best tradition of Adam Smith and apparently had been since pre-Spanish times. The question he asked was, If these people have such freedom, why aren't they rich? The answer he suggested was that significant wealth creation takes much more than just freedom from constraints. It requires the complex institutional development of a market society. In Guatemalan native society the modern firm had not yet developed, nor had any corresponding productive technology. The unit of production was the family.

The distinction between firm and family is crucial. Firms are impersonal in the sense that they have specialized, well-defined goals, recruit on the basis of ability and experience, and are single-mindedly market oriented. Families, on the other hand, have necessarily complex agendas in which, for example, recreation might rank high. They can neither recruit or fire except in a limited way through marriage or divorce or by recognizing extended family ties. They must accommodate old Aunt Flora and irascible Cousin John.

Manorial arrangements were family ventures and very unbusinesslike from today's perspective. The modern entrepreneurial community can accomplish infinitely more than the medieval manor because of its more evolved nature and because it operates in an altogether different environment, a competitive global economy of specialized firms including interlocking and supportive financial and service institutions of every description. We would make a mistake by attempting to understand the whole of the entrepreneurial community in terms of the medieval manor or the tribal village.

7. What will keep the managers of entrecoms from becoming tyrants?

Look around you, and what do you see? If we searched the records of the hundreds of thousands of entrecoms extant today, we might find some horror stories, but they would be exceptional and short lived. Years ago I conducted a field study of what kinds of dispute situations arise in mobile home parks and shopping centers and how they are handled (1971). In the course of the study I collected many entertaining case histories, but none was a horror story. The fact is that businesspeople for the most part look out for their customers. That's why they remain in business. If they get lax, someone else may buy the business and restore its profitability.

By contrast, we don't have to wonder a great deal about political communities. We know what to expect there. But no one should expect perfect consistency in either category. Even heaven had its Lucifer. What counts is the characteristic behavior we can expect of business enterprise, which is premised on service, as contrasted with piratical enterprise, which is by its nature predatory. Either one may step out of character on occasion, but such exceptions only point up the rule.

8. How will global decision-making take place?

I envision a deployment worldwide of small, autonomous communities not unlike what are called in anthropology "acephalous" or "stateless" societies, all cooperating rather informally at various levels by networking. For this view I am indebted to the late anthropologist Virginia H. Hine (1977, 1984).

9. But isn't profit the incentive driving all of this?

Yes, it's business incentive, and that is what makes it self-sustaining and enduring. Commerce is greatly undervalued and underestimated. The great and growing trend is for land to be administered as productive capital, and in the process what we are witnessing is a natural evolution of leasehold land tenures—exactly what Henry George, Ralph Borsodi, and others proposed as the cure for excessive speculation in land. But they didn't see that cure coming about as a spontaneous market process, powered by ordinary business incentive. It is strange that no one before Spencer Heath ever anticipated it happening this way.

10. Why will this change come about quickly instead of over a long period?

We know from history that when conditions are right for a new kind of development, that development can happen very rapidly. In this case we need only recall the crucial role of numbers in enabling us to develop science and commerce, and then observe that something spectacular is happening now. The advent of computers has increased our ability to manipulate not only numbers but information of all kinds by orders of magnitude, and this capability is progressing at an exponential rate. Moreover, the modem and personal computer, by making the home office a viable alternative to "downtown," is empowering individuals and enabling an exodus from the regimentation of the workforce, a decentralization within the marketplace of truly awe-inspiring magnitude.

For this reason among others I wouldn't be surprised to see

the entrepreneurial community pattern become general by the second quarter of the next century. At that time, should this development have occurred, we will not have overthrown but, without fanfare, will simply have outgrown government as we know it today. Government personnel will have moved into new, more productive employment. Human society, which I believe on the tribal level manifested the normal, healthy societal pattern albeit at an immature stage, will have matured and come into its own. Humankind finally will have negotiated what it may long look back upon as a difficult and hazardous riser in the stair of societal evolution.

References

Dove, Patrick Edward. [1850] 1910. *The Theory of Human Progression*. New York: Isaac H. Blanchard.

Foldvary, Fred. 1995. *Public Goods and Private Communities: The Market Provision of Social Services*. London: Edward Elgar.

Heath, Spencer. 1936. *Politics versus Proprietorship*. Privately printed 1957. *Citadel, Market and Altar*. Elkridge, Md.: Science of Society Foundation.

Hine, Virginia H. 1977. "The Basic Paradigm of a Future Socio-Cultural System." *World Issues*, April–May, 19–22, 1984. "Networks in a Global Society." *The Futurist*, June, 11–13.

Howard, Ebenezer. 1898. *Tomorrow: A Peaceful Path to Real Reform*. London: Swann Sonnenschein, [1902] 1965. *Garden Cities of Tomorrow*. Cambridge: MIT Press.

Jacobs, Jane. 1992. "Jasper and Kate on the Guardian Syndrome." Chap. 5 in *Systems of Survival: A Dialogue on the Moral Foundations of Commerce and Politics*. New York: Random House.

MacCallum, Spencer H. 1970. *The Art of Community*. Menlo Park,CA: Institute for Humane Studies.

———. 1971. "Jural Behavior in American Shopping Centers." In *Human Organization, Journal of the Society for Applied Anthropology* 30 (Spring): 3–10.

———.1996. "A Model Lease for Orbis." *Formulations* 3 (3), 16–23.

Maine, Sir Henry Sumner. [1861] 1986. *Ancient Law*. London: Dorset.

Ogilvie, William. [1782] 1970. *Birthright in Land—An Essay on the Right of Property in Land*. New York: Augustus M. Kelley.

Osborne, F. J. 1946. *Greenbelt Cities*. London: Faber and Faber.

Purdom, C. B. 1949. *The Building of Satellite Towns*. London: J. M. Dent.

Spence, Thomas. [1775] 1920. "The Real Rights of Man." In *Pioneers of Land Reform*, edited by M. Beer. London: G. Bells.

Spencer, Herbert. [1851] 1969. "The Right to the Use of the Earth." Chap. 9 in *Social Statics*. New York: Augustus M. Kelley.

Tax, Sol. 1972. Reprint. *Penny Capitalism: A Guatemalan Indian Economy*. New York: Octagon Books. Original edition, Smithsonian Institution: Institute of Social Anthropology 1953, Publication no. 16, 1953.

Whitehead, Alfred North. [1933] 1967. *Adventures of Ideas*. New York: The Free Press.

12

"The Enterprise of Community: Social and Environmental Implications of Administering Land as Productive Capital" (2003, rev. 2007)

We hear a lot of expressed concern about *conserving* the environment. But no one talks much about *producing* it. Why not manufacture it competitively and sell it in the free market like other goods and services—and even bundle it with product support? As a matter of fact, exactly that is being done. Designer environment is relatively new on the market, but its manufacturers stand behind it, and we will doubtless be seeing much more of it in the future.

To explain this unlikely sounding proposition, I shall first analyze an incentive structure that is only now gaining explicit recognition in commercial real estate. Then I shall describe a two-hundred-year empirical trend to show how the above scenario is being played out. In light of the incentives coming into play, this historic trend has some far-reaching and unexpected social implications.

It does not matter that the incentive structure I am about to describe is in its infancy, for in matters of social progress, it is always the trend and not any particular stage of development that is significant. But before tracing out the logic of these incentives, a key term calls for definition. For a moment let us talk abstractly about *land*.

Land as an Economic Concept

We are used to thinking of land as something physical; we describe it as clear, rocky, fertile or barren. But those who deal in land say that three things give it value: location, location, and location. It makes sense from an economic standpoint, therefore, to look at land not as anything physical but as a special kind of location having to do only incidentally with geophysical coordinates. It is intangible, always changing, never fixed in supply. I am talking about location with respect to all of the things in the environs of a site, near or far, present or anticipated, that have any relevance for its intended use. This excludes features of the site itself, such as the presence or absence of valuable minerals, soil, water, or built improvements. We are interested in what surrounds the site, not what is on it. Admittedly, having said that, the physical attributes of a site can influence the uses of surrounding land and, to that extent, its environment and hence its value. But except for that, the physical features just named can be bought, sold, altered, or removed from a site without affecting its *location* as here understood.

From this perspective, what landowners actually sell—that which commands value—is location with respect to a specific *environment* at the moment of consideration or anticipated for the future. A site merely defined by geophysical coordinates without reference to its surroundings has no ascertainable value; it comes into demand only as its environs have relevance for an activity that is to take place there. A prospective home site for a young family gains in desirability if there is a school nearby, or a mine site if there is a railroad accessible to transport its ores, or a retail site if there are residences nearby, not to mention parking spaces, utility grids and many other things. When we buy or sell land, therefore, we are trading in what might be called *positioning rights*—rights to position ourselves and our activities strategically relative to other people and activities we consider significant.

For this discussion, therefore, "land" will mean *economic location*, or location that is potentially of use to somebody so that it commands a market value. It should be noted that "location" in this sense and "environment" are correlative terms; each implies the other and by itself has no meaning. While it is practical to define a parcel of land in terms of "metes and bounds," or geophysical coordinates, because these are constant, its economic location and hence its value is fluid, reflecting the changing location/environment of the site and the subjectivity and situation of the actors. Paul Birch (2002) puts it succinctly in economic terms: "The site value of a property is simply the sum of the externalities directed to that property from all other properties."

Administering Land as Productive Capital

The immediate advantage an owner can take of his parcel of land is to use it himself, directly, as a farmer might or a homeowner. But that is of no interest to us here. Our concern is with the incentives a landowner acquires who brings his land into the market—that is to say, who sells or lets out its use to others. If he sells it, then of course he will be out of the picture and of no further interest for this particular discussion. But if he opts to lease it to others while retaining its ownership, he may be in the picture for a very long time. He will no longer be using the property himself, but will have made a specialty of its ownership and administration. Ownership and use will have separated. That is the situation we want to study—and the more so if he has multiple tenants. In the case of a single tenant, the discussion that follows may have little relevance. But with multiple tenants it begins to be consequential, because a multi-tenant property begins to approach a community.

When ownership and use have parted and the owner no longer has the direct use of his land, what is his incentive with respect to it? How can he maximize his advantage from it over the long term? The only way he can do so is by making the site more valuable to its present or prospective tenants/users so that it will bring more rent. What does that entail?

As suggested above, the use anyone makes of a site is facilitated—indeed made possible—by the suitability of the site for the activity in question. That suitability depends on what people are doing elsewhere, and the proposed activity, or lack of one, in turn affects the value of sites elsewhere, creating a systemic process constantly changing with changing culture, people, and technology. By modifying the environment of a site (and correspondingly its economic location) in ways that make the site better suited for its intended range of uses, landowners make it more valuable to present or prospective tenants—who are then able and willing to bid more for it.

What is significant in the broad social picture is that landlords singly and collectively—persons specialized in the ownership and administration of sites rather than in their use—have incentive to optimize the environment for present and prospective site users, in the process creating land value and helping to harmonize land uses community-wide. They are, collectively, the natural market agency of community land-use coordination and planning. They have an economic incentive to become environmental entrepreneurs.

The owner of a regional shopping mall, for example, is concerned about all of the things he has any control over within that mall that are environmentally significant for the individual leased sites, such as there being the right combination of stores to create maximum draw from the market area served—taking into account the income level, culture and special needs of that particular market. He is also concerned that the managers of those stores make up an effective retailing team, each ready to cooperate in a hundred different ways, such as participating in joint promotions, referring customers, maintaining a good appearance, keeping regular hours, or alerting one another promptly in security matters. He is equally concerned about having adequate parking and attractive landscaping of common areas.

But as a competent environmentalist, he is also concerned with a wide range of things *outside* his mall that affect each and every one of the sites he offers for lease within. He is of course concerned about the more obvious things, like convenient freeways and other transportation to the mall from his market area. But he also wants the community itself to be affluent—since that means a prosperous customer base for his mall merchants.

As within the mall itself, so in the surrounding community: one of the things most affecting the utility and value of land and thereby the affluence of inhabitants is the presence or absence of common services such as the provision and maintenance of parks and well-placed streets, water and power and other utilities, sewerage, security, justice services, and the like. Just as a mall owner, therefore, is concerned with the quality of management within his mall, so is he concerned with the quality of management in the community surrounding the mall, which is to say, the *quality of local government*. He is not alone in his concern. He is one among a growing constituency of commercial property owners, all of them concerned to see that municipal services are performed and performed well, whether that means monitoring, informally supervising, subsidizing, or actually providing the services—alone or in collaboration.

Now a small landlord, leasing or renting to perhaps one tenant, has little hope of improving or rearranging the environment of that small parcel to make it more valuable to the tenant. He is almost as helpless as an individual owner who uses the land directly. He lets it for whatever use and level of use the existing surroundings permit and has little control over how community infrastructure is provided. If he looks for any improvement at all, it is for municipal government to intervene on his behalf.

But as he enlarges his holding or combines with others to achieve a holding of more practical size, and begins to lease not to one but to multiple tenants, he gains leverage over the environment. He may now find it economically feasible and in his interest to build substantial physical infrastructure for tenants in a multi-tenant property. But even before that, he finds that he creates environment in the very act of leasing to multiple tenants, since each tenant becomes a factor in the environment of every other. This has been carried to high levels of sophistication in the selection and arrangement of tenants in shopping malls.

Returning to the example of the shopping mall landlord, he goes well beyond merely selecting and arranging particular land users for optimal synergy and then building physical infrastructure for them. By providing proactive leadership and by creating in the terms of his leases rules that facilitate community living, he builds effective *social* infrastructure as well. He brings focused attention to the myriad environmental factors affecting land users in that place in order to facilitate a highly complex, interactive community of landlord and merchant tenants.

Just as environment is blind to property lines, so is the landlord's concern on his tenants' behalf. As he achieves success in building land value, he becomes economically more able to influence environmental factors well beyond his property boundaries, both directly and in cooperation with other landlords, each of whom has similar environmental concerns.

By virtue of this incentive, a distinctive entrepreneurial role for landowners in the market place has been building for more than two centuries. Instead of continuing like everyone else on his own plot as an environmental consumer, some owners have specialized and differentiated by administering their land to benefit others, who now have become their customers. In so doing, they are administering land as *productive capital in the market*. Their enterprise consists in the production and marketing of optimal human environment. As this enterprise has grown, so has the accompanying know-how.

However unconscious and unplanned, the spread of this enterprise reveals the general outline of a new paradigm of incentives governing the production and distribution of community goods. Ever so quietly, little remarked by social commentators but with the seeming inevitability of a sea change, this new paradigm has made its appearance with the advent and growth of multi-tenant income properties in every area of commercial real estate.

Growth of Multi-Tenant Income Properties

The multi-tenant income property (MIP) is the application in an urban setting of a form of land tenure that for millennia characterized agrarian societies. It consists in holding the overall land title intact while parceling sites among land users by leasing. Site improvements, on the other hand, may be owned by anyone, depending on the particular circumstances. Multi-tenant income properties are the antithesis of real-estate subdivisions, such as condominiums and planned unit developments, in which a tract of land is fragmented into many separate ownerships.

Although the principle is ancient and widespread, modern multi-tenant income properties stand out as an American phenomenon. From their first appearance in the second quarter of the nineteenth century, they grew along a rising trend line that steepened after World War II, when they began to expand dramatically in number, kind, size, and complexity.[55] Entrepreneurs in this new line of business created myriad environments reflecting the specialized needs of a seemingly endless variety of clientele—merchants, travelers, manufacturers, residents, and professionals of every variety. Each new type of environment that met with success in the market defined an economic niche. In rapid succession, we saw the debut of hotels, apartment buildings, office buildings ("skyscrapers"), luxury liners, camping grounds, commercial airports, shopping centers, recreational vehicle (RV) parks, mobile home parks, coliseums, small-craft marinas, research parks, professional parks, medical clinics, theme parks, leasehold manufactured home communities, as well as, increasingly, integrations and combinations of these and others to form properties larger, more complex and, significantly, less narrowly specialized.

As these properties become more generalized through mixed, complementary uses, they begin to approach what we are accustomed to think of as communities. Some hotels today, for example, compare with a small but complex city. The Venetian Hotel in Las Vegas, for example, includes shopping malls, professional offices, convention facilities, restaurants and cafes, chapels, theaters and art galleries, medical services, a security force, and the list goes on. In terms of population size, counting registered guests, visitors, and service personnel, it is two to three times larger on any given day than was the city of Boston at the time of the Revolutionary War.[56]

As entrepreneurial landowners learned to build land value by optimizing environment for land users, a major segment of the business community in the United States abandoned the atomistic pattern of subdivided lots along Main Street, devoid of a unifying proprietary interest, and moved onto larger landholdings organized and managed under integrated ownership. Here the organized landowners—of whom there can be unlimited numbers through the use of stock and other undivided interests—provide many of the services that once only governments provided, including streets and parking, sewerage, storm drainage, power distribution, policing, and landscaped public places. Indeed, the sophistication of common goods now routinely provided in large multi-tenant income properties has far surpassed that of municipalities.

The rapidity of growth of such environmental enterprise in the free market was extraordinary. The shopping center at the close of World War II was small and experimental. Fewer than a dozen existed in the United States, and the name had yet to be coined. Today, shopping centers and malls in the United States number 47,000 and accommodate half of the non-automotive retail activity of the nation (ICSC 2001).[57]

Landlords have far transcended their stereotypical role. From being merely passive recipients of rents, they have become entrepreneurs. For each specialized type of multi-tenant property, they have tailored their management style to the needs of their clients. A large mall, for example, requires a serious commitment to leadership on the part of management to forge a collection of merchant tenants into an effective retailing team. Teams need a coach, and the mall manager is it. His coaching role calls for keeping the peace and building morale among highly competitive merchants (MacCallum 1971). The merchants recognize his unique qualifications. His concentrated entrepreneurial interest in the land confers on him qualities found nowhere else in the mall. Unlike the tenants he serves, who are naturally partisan and inclined to exploit the mall as a commons, he is at once interested and disinterested. His personal and business interest is in the success of the mall as such and therefore in the success of each and every proprietor on the team. This leadership presence in the shopping mall is a major environmental asset for the community of merchants. Commentators in the retail trade literature have called it the whole premise of the shopping center.

Rationale of the Multi-Tenant Income Property

The business rationale of the multi-tenant income property is straightforward. As environmental entrepreneurs in the economic niche defined by their type of property compete to lower their asking rents, a field of prospective tenants, similarly competing, bid up the rents they are willing to pay. For owners and managers who succeed in offering attractive physical and social environment in this competitive market, land revenues return the costs and a profit besides.

Multi-tenant income properties are essentially communities. As such, they stand out against the tragic record of traditional, subdivided communities, which can only be run politically. Subdivisions are not market phenomena because they do not sell a product and consequently have no customers. Hence they generate no income, but must subsist on assessments, or tax levies. Multi-tenant income properties, on the other hand, are business enterprises. Because they serve customers, they earn an income. Their market revenue makes them self-supporting— and more than merely self-supporting. Market revenue not only finances the current operation, it enables the accumulation of reserve funds from which to renovate as needed or even to completely rebuild to the same or another use in that or another location to stay competitive with other locations being similarly administered in the market. This illustrates the immortality of productive capital.

A natural question arises regarding the growth and spread of multi-tenant income properties. Why, with the major exception of apartments and hotels, has nothing comparable happened in the housing field?[58] Instead, we have subdivisions with homeowners' associations, which David Friedman (1987,506) describes as government like any other.[59] The anomaly may be due to a combination of factors. A partial explanation may be that innovations often appear first in the business world, where competition drives innovation and efficiency, and later make their way into the consumer market. A different explanation is cultural—the longstanding ideological bias in America favoring home ownership over renting or leasing that traces to colonial times and the repudiation of the last vestiges of feudalism in Europe. Still another explanation is public policy. Detached, single-family subdivision housing has been aggressively promoted since the 1930s by a collaboration of the federal government with the corporate building industry.[60] In addition, federal income tax policy discriminates against renting or leasing for residential use. The federal government also directly subsidizes homeownership through its various federal mortgage insurance programs. The fact that such insurance only covers homes in a subdivision with a qualifying homeowners' association in effect mandates subdivision housing, since most builders feel their product must qualify for federal insurance if they are to remain competitive in the industry. Added to these various federal requirements, the taxing of dividends at substantially higher rates than capital gains (at top rates the difference is 39.5 percent versus 20 percent) encourages short-term venturing for capital gain, as in subdivision housing, over conservative, long-term investment for income. At the local level, many municipalities require residential developers to adhere to the formula of subdivision with a mandatory-membership homeowners' association.

Certainly all of these factors play a role, but understanding how they are to be weighed one against another awaits empirical and historical study. The public policy factor is so great as to suggest that the ubiquity of subdivision over land leasing in residential housing may be a matter of market distortion more than of consumer preference. To the extent the explanation is cultural and psychological, we do know from the abrupt shift of New York City apartment living from disrepute to respectability almost overnight in the mid-nineteenth century that such change can happen rapidly (Cromley 1990).

Social Implications

However they may be provided, it is important to recognize that common services and amenities like streets, utilities, parks and public safety pertain to sites rather than to individuals as such; individuals derive benefit from them only as occupants of a place. Thus when landowners sell or lease sites for price or rent, they are in fact acting as the market purveyor of the public services and other environmental amenities attaching to that place.

With that in mind, we can readily imagine a scenario forecast by Spencer Heath in 1936. Pointing out that communities have owners, albeit unorganized, he forecast that the growing class of entrepreneurial landlords, representing broad segments of the investing public, would organize and begin to monitor the provision of public services. In so doing they would become thoroughly aware of the fact that they are merchandisers of the environmental amenities of their combined sites and that, prominent among these, are the public services of the host community. In a strict sense therefore, he argued, public employees act [as] agents of the owners of the land of the community, even if the latter do not fully pay or supervise them.

Today, Heath continued, the unorganized owners of a community might be likened to the owners of a hotel who allow their staff to be chosen by public shout and, without any supervision or salary, to finance themselves and the operation as they see fit by picking the pockets of the guests. But as enterprising landowners become aware of their role in the provision and marketing the public goods—how they fit into the larger societal picture—it will only remain for a sufficient number of them to organize and assume full responsibility for servicing the community, which will then become a market enterprise. First they would voluntarily assume full fiscal responsibility, realizing in a practical way the Georgist dream of the "single tax," followed in due course by administrative responsibility. This, Heath forecast, will all come about as a matter of good business. Commercial landowners will see their opportunity to enhance land values dramatically by providing effective community services while relieving site users of the harassment and burden on their productivity that taxation and bureaucratic regulation entail.[61] The provision of common goods will then become a truly competitive market enterprise.

Robert Nisbet (1952) in his classic, *The Quest for Community*, described the importance, for the preservation of freedom, of "intermediate associations" of many kinds—familial, religious, economic, professional, recreational, academic—acting as buffers between individuals and political government. Because of their immature development when he was writing toward the close of World War II, it did not occur to him to specify multi-tenant income properties as a prime example of what he was describing. Later (1991), he acknowledged the omission, observing that they "assuredly fit the category of intermediate associations and perhaps also communities."

The manager of a shopping-center in a small California city volunteered how multi-tenant income properties provide such buffering. A large part of his role as manager, he said, was running interference between the local city government and his merchants so that they could devote more of their time to operating their business, to their own profit and to that of the center as a whole. He said he participated widely in civic organizations in the host community "to make friends for the center" and knew "the right people to get something done, as long as it's fair." He cited examples of the center's cooperation with civic clubs, schools, and the Boy Scouts, and counted as personal friends the mayor, city manager, chief of police, and fire chief (MacCallum 1971).

If we make but the single assumption that the historic trend toward the business-like administration of land as productive capital will continue, then it seems inevitable from the logic of the situation that the growing numbers of owners of multi-tenant income properties will associate to further their common interests, and that at the top of the list will be the shared desire to enhance community-wide services while relieving land users of taxation and its abuses and reducing bureaucratic regulation. Historically, being small and divided, landowners had little power to effect any significant improvements outside their own small parcel. The increase in the number and size of commercial holdings, however, and the growing involvement of the investing public, is changing that picture.

As such trade associations develop, their membership will come to include not only larger landowning interests, but also owners of small multi-tenant and single-tenant properties and even owner-occupiers, as these associations are seen to offer a more promising avenue to improvements than city hall. For the first time ever, we will see major trade groups endowed with substantial resources dedicated to promoting the public interest. For the special interest of their founding member firms will be the prosperity and well being of their tenants and properties, which they will see as interconnected with and dependent upon that of the host community.

As local real estate associations grow and develop and

communities prosper, the environmental industry will inevitably organize on state and regional levels and take on correspondingly broader responsibilities for the physical and social environment. Associations will concern themselves with regional security, public parklands, and communications, even as shopping malls today on a small scale are known to build public roads and other common facilities, pro-rating the costs between them.

Fully half-a-century before modern multi-tenant income properties appeared in the United States, Adam Smith described the congruence he saw between the landed interest and the general public interest. In ways he could not have foreseen, the present discussion bears out his statement of broad principle:

> The interest [of landowners] is strictly and inseparably connected with the general interests of the society. Whatever either promotes or obstructs the one, necessarily promotes or obstructs the other. When the public deliberates concerning any regulation of commerce or police, the proprietors of land never can mislead it, with a view to promote the interest of their own particular order; at least, if they have any tolerable knowledge of that interest.

This alignment of the landed interests with the interests of land users, the latter embracing the whole of society, is explained by the fact that land utility and value is a function of environment. As an economy becomes more specialized, this concert of interests becomes ever more marked. When an individual gives up the direct use of his land and instead administers it as productive capital by letting its use to others, he acquires an economic interest in creating environments conducive to the well being of those others. His concern extends, albeit indirectly, to the total population, since its well being or adversity in turn affects his tenants.

It is noteworthy that Spencer Heath more than half-a-century ago was not so much proposing a social reform as he was merely predicting a future course of events, extrapolating from the market process as he understood it from what he saw happening around him. If the scenario he forecast is correct, the commercial real estate industry will find it in its business interest to voluntarily assume the full provision of public services, both locally and regionally. Not the least of these services will be to untax land users and relieve them of the manifold burdens of political government. In this way will the industry promote the general prosperity while building land values for its investors throughout the population. Through local and regional realty associations, neighborhood will compete with neighborhood, community with community, and region with region. On all of these levels, the competitive provision of common goods will be among the most highly profitable of all enterprises.

Conclusion

At the beginning of this paper, I set out to get the reader's attention by stating an unlikely sounding proposition. I said that human environment, both social and physical, resembles any other good or service in that it is amenable to being manufactured, marketed and maintained through the freely competitive processes of the market. I then did three things. I analyzed how this works in theory, described how it has evolved in practice, and showed the unexpected and significant result toward which the practice must logically lead.

That is to say, I first analyzed an incentive structure that was not present so long as land was mainly owned for consumption or speculation, but that came about with the emergence of land ownership as a capital enterprise. Second, I showed how that pattern has unfolded historically in the emergence and proliferation of modern multi-tenant income properties. Finally, from that trend in real estate, I extrapolated to the future.

The unexpected result logically implied by the continuation of this trend in real estate is nothing less than the qualitative transformation of government from, to follow Oppenheimer's distinction set out in *The State*, a *political* process to one purely *economic*. It seems especially fitting that this transformation will come about not by taxation, the marching and marshalling of armies, or the deliberations of legislative bodies, but by the quiet emergence of the *enterprise of community* as an almost incidental consequence of the continued normal development of the market process.

References

Paul Birch, "A critique of Georgism," August 29, 2002, http://www.paulbirch.net.

Elizabeth Cromley, *Alone Together: A History of New York's Early Apartments* (Ithaca: Cornell University Press, 1990).

David Friedman, "Comment: Problems in the provision of public goods," *Harvard Journal of Law and Public Policy*, Vol. 10 (1987).

Spencer Heath, *Citadel, Market and Altar* (Baltimore: Science of Society Foundation 1957).

Spencer Heath, *Politics versus Proprietorship* (Elkridge, MD: Privately printed, 1936). International Council of Shopping Centers (www.ICSC.org), ScopeUSA, 2001.

Spencer H. MacCallum, "Residential politics: How democracy erodes community," *Critical Review* Vol. 17 Nos. 3–4 (Fall/Winter 2005), pp. 393–425.

Spencer H. MacCallum, "Jural behavior in American shopping centers: Initial views of the proprietary community," *Human Organization: Journal of the Society for Applied Anthropology* 30:1 (spring 1971).

Spencer H. MacCallum, *The Art of Community* (Menlo Park, CA: Institute for Humane Studies, 1970).

Evan McKenzie, *Privatopia: Homeowner Associations and the Rise of Residential Private Government* (Yale University Press, 1994).

Robert A. Nisbet, Letter to the writer (on file) dated October 21, 1991.

Robert A. Nisbet, *The Quest for Community*. (London: Oxford Press, 1952).

Adam Smith, *The Wealth of Nations* (New York: P. F. Collier and Son, 1901), part 1.

"The Enterprise of Community: Social and Environmental Implications of Administering Land as Productive Capital." *Journal of Libertarian Studies* 17, no. 4 (Fall 2003). Ludwig von Mises Institute, www.mises.org/journals.asp. Revised by the author in 2007. https://explorersfoundation.org/archive/28ot1-maccallum-ec.pdf.

13

"Freedom's Ugly Duckling: A Fresh Take on Private Property in Land" (2015)

This paper was presented at the Mises Austrian Economic Research Conference 2016 at Auburn, Alabama, April 2. A slightly earlier version was published in Libertarian Papers 7, no. 2 (2015): 135-55. It is subject to a Creative Commons Attribution 3.0 License.

Abstract: The writer offers historic reasons for the paucity of public and academic discussion of private property in land. He emphasizes the importance of the separation of land and state that took place in the 18th and 19th centuries, a separation that, without better understanding of the social function of property in land, is in danger of being lost. He attributes Henry George's and Karl Marx's destructive attacks on property in land to lack of such understanding and uncritical acceptance of Locke's labor theory of ownership. F. A. Harper urged the importance of new social insights and founded the Institute for Humane Studies expressly to create an intellectual environment conducive to breakthroughs in scientific thinking about society. Spencer Heath's operationalizing two basic concepts of social science, "property" and "capital," was such a breakthrough. The one avoids the Lockean problem, and the other helps make sense of a little remarked but massive sea change over the past century in the United States from the administration of land by owners for their own exclusive use to administration of land for the benefit of others as productive capital in multi-tenant properties. This trend has implications for further social evolution in which we may very likely see public services provided contractually in the free market instead of by taxation.

PROPERTY IN LAND has long been a problem for classical liberals and libertarians if not, for many, a downright embarrassment. Since the time of Henry George more than a century ago, it has been charged with being the one instance in economics where there is truly a free lunch—land owners enjoying a free ride by collecting rents for doing nothing. This, if true, smacks more of a political than a free-market phenomenon—of privilege rather than property. Yet we do call land "property," and we freely buy and sell it. What is it, then? Is it an artificial creature of the state, a form of state-imposed privilege like taxi licenses in New York City? Or is it authentic property, a social institution prior to and independent of all legislation? Classical liberals traditionally oppose privilege and defend property. Yet given this ambiguity, is it any wonder that, with a few notable exceptions, they have had little to say about property in land, either pro or con?[62] To help remedy this lack of attention and hopefully encourage scholars to take a fresh look at property in land, I shall do three things: trace some historical reasons for its poor image; explain the essential social function a land owner performs; and offer some empirical reasons why private property in land is arguably freedom's ugly duckling that in time may become its white swan.

I. How the Stage Was Set

Historically the stage was set by the close association of land ownership with political government. In most of Europe before the eighteenth century, land and state were as one. Whatever political power there was, land owners exercised it. While not the case worldwide, this was true of most of Europe. The revolutions of the eighteenth and nineteenth centuries, however, brought about a distinct separation of land and state.[63] Due to whatever happy circumstances, the nobility found themselves stripped of political authority without being dispossessed of their lands. Political power was taken from them, but land titles were left largely intact. The law courts then struck down the many feudal restraints on the buying and selling of land, restraints such as primogeniture and entail, leaving land as freely exchangeable in the market as anything else.

But the stigma of land ownership from its association with political power survived long after the revolutions that overthrew the old order. No doubt it was this stigma that made John Stuart Mill and many other classical liberals distrustful of the institution. But also, they had less reason to study land than they once might have, since in their day commerce and industry, born of the industrial revolution, were surpassing agriculture in productivity and taking center stage as the significant producers of wealth and public revenue.

Locke's Labor Theory

A theoretical issue would further confuse the question of land as property. Private property in land was not reconcilable with

Locke's labor theory of ownership. This attracted little if any attention at the time, but it became apparent later. Had it not been for the general classical-liberal suspicion of and lack of interest in land, the theoretical issue might have been addressed and solved. But, as it happened, it was ignored. Let's look back to Locke's time for perspective.

With the first significant growth of commerce and industry in England, a fledgling middle class had begun to emerge, and this fact did not long escape the notice of the king and his tax collectors. In the resulting growing conflict with the monarch, who justified his rule by an impressive theory of divine right, the middle class needed a countering doctrine. They found it in an alternate doctrine of right that had been lying about, not much used, since the time of Cicero and, before him, the Greek Stoics. This was a theory not of divine right, but of "natural" rights, or rights according to reason. Natural rights theory said a person has a property in his life, from which it follows that he must also have a right to own property in things needful to sustain his life. So far so good.

John Locke, influenced by Cicero, became the principal theoretician of the middle class in their confrontation with the monarchy. Out of a proper regard for his own life, he kept this role secret, hiding for a time his authorship of his famed *Second Treatise on Government* (1691) even from his family.[64] He elaborated the natural rights doctrine, giving the middle class a powerful argument very much like the king's own claim to divine right, but substituting nature for God. But then, building on this, Locke went a step further and propounded a special argument to justify private property of all kinds. This was his labor theory of ownership, which held that property is made by "mixing one's labor" with something not previously owned.

Thus property, he said, being compounded of one's labor and thereby being an extension of one's personality, or self, comes under protection of the same natural right as life itself.

Bear in mind that the middle class was chiefly made up of people to whom the notion of "mixing labor" had direct appeal; they were laboring people, manufacturers and traders, rather than land owners whose principal wealth came from rents. Moreover, the doctrine served them well in their struggle with the king. No one was inclined, therefore, to look too deeply or critically into this appealing idea.

The theoretical problem was this: since land and natural resources, not being man-made, do not fit the labor theory of ownership, does that mean that land is not property? Thinkers of the day were not really concerned; because they chiefly represented the bourgeoisie rather than the landed interest, they cared little for land owners and devoted little time to thinking about the matter. But others eventually would.

The logical inference from the labor theory of ownership was that if land is not property, yet is bought and sold as such, then it must be something else masquerading as property. That something else could only be monopoly privilege enforced by the state. Remove that enforcement and presumably, unlike authentic property, which is social and customary, property in land would not stand but would atrophy and fall away.

Karl Marx and Henry George were two who accepted the idea of land not being property and took Locke's labor theory to its logical conclusion by demanding that the "privilege" be abolished. The first plank of the Communist Manifesto of 1848[65] called for the abolition of property in land, and this remains a prime tenet of Marxism. The greatest exponent of this view, however, was Henry George, whose plan in effect was to tax ownership of land out of existence. "Justice the Object—Taxation the Means" was how he titled one of his pamphlets.[66]

Henry George was a man of contradictions, in many respects socialist, in other respects not. He was without question the most compelling writer and orator on behalf of free trade who ever lived. At the same time, his position on land went far toward making Marxism credible.[67] His forceful crusade against property in land caught the attention of the world like a meteor, entraining vast numbers to the cause, including such luminaries of the day as Leo Tolstoy, Winston Churchill, Sun Yat-sen, Theodore Roosevelt, Louis Brandeis, John Dewey, Herbert Spencer (for a time), Albert Einstein, Helen Keller, and Woodrow Wilson. But in 1897, at the height of his crusade, Henry George suffered a fatal stroke and died, embroiled in the heat of a political campaign, which he seemed to be winning, to become mayor of New York City. Nevertheless, his message was clear: land ownership is unjust.

The intense controversy aroused by George faded not long after his death. Not understanding the functional role of private property in land and therefore able to pose only normative points of view and questions of practicality, both sides finally exhausted their arguments without any closure. So public discussion of property in land was muted during much of the twentieth century. But the message of Henry George, always implicit in American mistrust of Europe's landed gentry and fueled by stories of tenement landlords, Western land grabs, and the Irish Question, now became explicit in American culture as never before. It manifested in such diverse ways as the popular game of Monopoly, designed by Georgists to teach the evils of landlordism, and perhaps more recently in the adoption of the phrase "rent-seeking" as a technical term in economics for attempting to get without giving.[68]

If Henry George's campaign, by undermining the legitimacy of property in land in the popular and academic mind, did not actually pave the way for a growing new pattern in United States politics, it did nothing to counteract it. The new pattern has been that of *undoing* the separation of land and state that was achieved some two centuries ago. This turn in American politics has been an integral part of the increase of governmental power throughout the twentieth and into the twenty-first century. A gradual but relentless resumption of political control over land has taken many forms such as zoning, urban planning and urban renewal, the broadening of eminent domain, national parks, wilderness areas, the worldwide promotion of "land reform," the environmental movement, the United Nations World Heritage Sites and Biosphere Reserves, and the expanding confrontations with respect to ranch lands in the Western states. Federal agencies, alone, control a third of the nation's dry land.[69] Ronald Reagan in 1983 proclaimed sovereign rights over 3.9 *billion* acres of "submerged lands" in the US Exclusive Economic Zone, the sea and sea beds out to 200 nautical miles offshore, including much of the Gulf of Mexico and immense amounts of the Pacific Ocean due to the military use of small islands during World War II—the "biggest land grab in US government history."[70]

The stakes are high. Because every imaginable human activity involves some land use, political control of the occupancy and use of land translates into control of people, and hence totalitarianism, not to mention foreclosing the possibility of making any rational economic allocation of natural resources. Resistance to the reunification of land and state has been weakened by hesitation on the part of proponents of freedom to close ranks on the issue. They seem to sense a need to defend private property in land, but given its ill repute and not understanding its social role, they are paralyzed, unable to mount a principled defense. Such inaction may be their undoing.

The failure to adequately address the nature of property in land on functional grounds has left an open avenue for ceding all control of land back to the state. In this latter-day fight with a monarchy, as it were, Locke's labor theory of ownership is worse than useless. Clearly what is needed is a new perspective, a fresh way of looking at the matter. Let's begin by reviewing the social function of ownership, which applies not just to land but to every form of property.

The Social Function of Ownership
In all the heated debates over the land question originating in Locke's labor theory of ownership, the social function of property in land was seldom if ever addressed. Yet the convention of ownership operates the same with land as with anything else.

Ownership is a largely tacit social consensus having little or nothing to do with legislated law, as evidenced by the elaborate development of systems of property in stateless societies.[71] It is found everywhere and cross-culturally, strongly suggesting that, like language, it is instinctual. Within the cooperating group, it seems to be as natural for humans to evolve systems of ownership as for birds to build nests. Not only does it enable resources to be used productively, the owners being secure in their use, it also and thereby enables resources to be gifted and traded—bought and sold—and hence markets to develop, moving resources into the hands of those who can pay the most and are thereby likely to be the most productive users, to the enrichment of society.

The practice of ownership allows the peaceable distribution and redistribution of secure access to scarce resources, land or any others, by voluntary exchange. It must never be confused with possession; for ownership is a social phenomenon, as mere possession is not. A chicken with something in its beak runs from the other chickens. A person, on the other hand, can leave his home for days at a time, knowing that neighbors will watch it as if it were their own. I once lived for a short time in a mobile-home park in Nevada, and when about to leave for a weekend, my newly befriended Hells' Angels–type neighbor volunteered, "Anybody mess with your rig, I'll save you the scalp."

Nor is ownership a relation between a person and a thing, as is possession. It is a relation between a person and all others in the cooperating group *with respect to* the thing. It is the largely tacit social authority granted a person to determine the use of something or to pass that authority to another or others. And that passing, not of the thing itself but of the social authority over it, the title to it, is a service that only an owner can perform. Such transfer of social authority is a social-psychological service, something the materialist Henry George, focusing on physical labor as the source of all wealth, did not comprehend. He failed to see how, as Manuel F. Ayau has so cogently shown, the purely psychological activity of voluntary exchange in and of itself creates wealth.[72]

But we have yet to answer the question: if the Lockean idea of ownership, crafted more than three centuries ago as the rallying cry of a special-interest group fighting the English crown, fails to serve us today, can we improve upon it?

II. Science and Observation
In 1956, F. A. "Baldy" Harper (1905–1973) was considering giving up his position at the Foundation for Economic Education (FEE)

because, however good FEE was at teaching what was already known about freedom and the free-market process, it gave no encouragement for innovative, or "growing edge" thinking. Baldy confided in his friend Spencer Heath (1876–1963) his dream of founding an organization—the Institute for Humane Studies— that might prepare the way for significant breakthroughs in the study of men and their social relations. Heath encouraged Baldy's dream, assisted him in planning and offered his hundred-acre country home, Roadsend Gardens, in Elkridge, Maryland as a campus.[73] The two looked forward to the emergence of an authentic science of human social behavior.[74] For if the mark of a successful science is its ability to generate dependable technology, then the world's worsening state of politics and war was prima facie evidence of something seriously lacking in the social sciences as practiced. Anticipating the development of an authentic social science, Baldy hoped to create in the Institute for Humane Studies a unique environment of inquiry that would be conducive to discovery.[75]

What might breakthroughs in the social sciences entail? Well, for one, science is first and last based upon observation. Secondly, science depends upon peer review and replication of results by others. This requires, at the least, communicating accurately one's observations, for consensus in science is only possible when all parties know with reasonable certainty that they are observing the same thing. How do we describe what it is that we are observing in such terms that others can be confident that they are observing the same thing we are?

Nobelist Percy Bridgman addresses exactly this question in physics. In *The Nature of Physical Theory*, he gives a lucid discussion of the need for operational definitions of the basic concepts of a science.[76] Operational definitions are such that anyone, by performing a certain number of specified procedures or operations, can communicate unambiguously the observation at hand despite differences of individual experience and expectations and subtleties of translation between languages and cultures.

Spencer Heath operationalized the terms "property" and "capital, which he considered fundamental for fruitful discussion of human social organization. Let us first consider "property," followed by a discussion of "capital."

Property

The word "property" has long been problematic in the lexicon of the social sciences. The utilitarian position of Hobbes, Montesquieu, and Bentham, that property ultimately is a creation of the state, conveys the atomistic, individualist, and even antisocial implications expressed by John R. Commons when he wrote that the price one pays for "food, clothing, shelter, or land . . . is the price paid for the right . . . to have the government exclude everybody else from the said food, clothing, shelter, or land."[77] But as we have seen, ownership consists of more than simply a person's claim, regardless of what she or he might invoke for justification. It has a social component. It is worlds apart from mere possession, which is physical and must be defended by the possessor. Far from holding things away from others, it is the means of bringing resources into secure use accessible to all on equal terms.

The fallacy of seeing ownership in the light of one individual while ignoring the social context was recognized as early as 1877 by T. E. Cliffe Leslie:

No mere psychological explanation of the origin of property is, I venture to affirm, admissible, though writers of great authority have attempted to discover its germs by that process in the lower animals. A dog, it has been said, shows an elementary proprietary sentiment when he hides a bone, or keeps watch over his master's goods. But property has not its root in the love of possession. All living beings like and desire certain things, and if nature has armed them with any weapons are prone to use them in order to get and keep what they want. What requires explanation is not the want or desire of certain things on the part of individuals, but the fact that other individuals, with similar wants and desires, should leave them in undisturbed possession, or allot to them a share, of such things. It is the conduct of the community, not the inclination of individuals, that needs investigation. The mere desire for particular articles, so far from accounting for settled and peaceful ownership, tends in the opposite direction, namely, to conflict and the right of the strongest. No small amount of error in several departments of social philosophy, and especially in political economy, has arisen from reasoning from the desires of the individual, instead of from the history of the community.[78]

Spencer Heath transcended the controversy by defining "property" in a way that clearly communicated his observation and made consensus possible among any number of people with respect to what it was they were looking at. He defined "property" as anything that can become the subject matter of contract:

Property may be anything that by the custom of society becomes the subject matter of ownership and thereby of the social, non-violent processes and relations called contract, between persons, with respect to its disposition or use.[79]

Implicit in this definition are all of the essential features of property enabling a person to enter with confidence into contracts with others.

We now have an operational definition based on specific behavior that can be observed. The difference in outlook is significant. The idea of property as an extension of one's life, to which one has a "right" somehow vouchsafed by nature, or reason, if not by God, and that one is thereby morally "entitled" to defend, is a good line to take when fighting with a monarch. Heath, on the other hand, observed the social behavior we call property as a naturalist might—first describing it, and then examining it in its context to understand how it contributes to maintaining the organization, or process, in which it occurs. Unlike Henry George, who crusaded for "justice" and looked to legislation to bring it about by force, Heath sought to understand and describe spontaneous social behavior as he found it.

So let us recapitulate for a moment. Ownership is worlds apart from mere animal possession, or territory, which an individual alone must defend. It also consists of more than merely a person's claim, regardless of what the claimant might invoke for justification. It has a social component.

The practice of ownership and thereby of property is a social covenant that is largely tacit, and consequently as little noted as the healthy functioning of our bodies tends to be. But curiously, some sense of it can be understood in terms of the several permutations of the English verb "to own"—which in the eighteenth century was the same word as "to owe." The parties to the covenant are *owners* not only because they as individuals claim a sole jurisdiction, to be observed by all, over certain specified resources, but because they *own*, or confess, or acknowledge—in the sense of "owning up"—that they owe the same courtesy to other owners with respect to their claims similarly made and socially acknowledged. They then stand as witness to similar claims of others and are prepared to defend those claims as if they were their own. The result is what Alvin Lowi felicitously calls a "covenantal community,"[80] prerequisite to human social living. The security of "quiet," or unchallenged, possession granted by the covenantal community makes it possible for a person to put aside his weapons and use productively a given resource for himself or to contract with others respecting it. Indeed, it is only by virtue of its secure possession making it accessible and usable that anything can become a resource. Only such can become the subject matter of contract. It is the covenantal, or social, authority over the resource that commands value in exchange. That, and not the resource itself, is the actual subject matter of the contract.

So, ownership is far from atomistic, as if individuals were negatively charged particles repelling one another or colliding and flying apart, each a threat to every other. If it were otherwise, people would not come together as we observe that they do. We observe that people don't fly apart but draw together into communities transcending even biologic kin groups. There is an innate attraction. It is through the psychological accord of ownership that they attract rather than repel. More than being an individual's claim against others, ownership is a boon, the blessing of quiet possession one receives from all others and owes to all others in the covenantal community.

To recapitulate, it is this psychological accord that makes it possible to come together peaceably and cooperate by exchanging; for only then does one have something durable—in the sense of something that can last—to offer. Mere possession is physical and precarious. Ownership on the other hand enables us to peaceably give and receive quiet possession of scarce goods or services by transferring social jurisdiction over them and thereby to enter into voluntary exchange, which is the beginning of society.

The beauty of this social-psychological accord is that it gives everyone not only security of possession, but a *transferable* security of possession. Thus it is not political government, as Hobbes thought, but the instinctual, wholly psychological, verging on unconscious, practice of ownership that resolves Hobbes' fearful dream of "war of all against all." Heath observed that this uniquely human means of securing and reconciling the uses of scarce resources is everywhere practiced in human society without distinction as to the kind of resource, whether natural or artifact. He found no human propensity to treat land and natural resources as a special case.

Changing Perception of Land

Having discussed at length the first term, "property," in the expression "property in land," I'll now give some attention to the second term, "land." Is land truly physical, finite, and not amenable to being created, as traditional Georgists hold, or is it in fact something intangible, unlimited, and capable of being produced and marketed? We can gain some needed perspective by recognizing how profoundly the evolving market economy since the time of Locke and, more recently, of Marx and Henry George has affected the perception of land itself.[81]

In the eighteenth century, most people were subsistence farmers, met most of their needs by their own effort, and had little traffic with the then still-rudimentary market process. They thought of land as a tillable field, a woodlot, or possibly a site for mining various natural resources. It gained value as they built up or imported richer soil or discovered minerals in it, and lost value as they exhausted the soil or the minerals. The French Physiocrats held that land was the source of all wealth. It was perceived as physical, the solid part of the earth's surface, and necessarily fixed in amount.

The market process then began rapidly evolving, to an extent unprecedented in human experience. By specializing their activities and exchanging their products and services, people found their wealth exponentially increasing. But with specialization, land uses were no longer uniform. Instead of each family using the soil much as their neighbors did, land uses became increasingly diverse. Now it became important how people located their activities relative to other land uses. All wanted proximity to their particular suppliers and markets, and so there was a booming growth of cities as people crowded in and jockeyed for the most strategic position vis-à-vis significant others. The development of a market in land enabled them to move about, positioning their specialized activities to best advantage relative to those of other people. Property rights in land can thus be described as positioning rights, and the buying and selling of land as the buying and selling of such rights. As fertility of soil ceased to be a major consideration for most, what mattered more was access to surrounding land uses and natural features, which is to say, the unique environment to which each site offered access. Where the Physiocrat might have quipped that "three things give land its value: fertility, fertility, and fertility," today's real estate broker says, "location, location, and location."

In this newer sense, land is altogether intangible, simply any location in the cosmos, identifiable by a three-dimensional address in space. But to be useful, and hence to have market value, it must for any given purpose be located strategically with respect to significant activities, present or prospective. Its value now depends on its economic location—not simply any location in the cosmos, but a location relative to present or prospective human activities. Such value is independent of any resource or activity on the parcel itself, except as that might influence change in surrounding activities and these then react back upon and affect the original value. Economic location, and with it land value, is ever changing, continually being destroyed and created, and constantly in flux as human activities change.[82]

Now we are talking about "land" in two different senses, the one older and quite physical, some part of the solid surface of the earth, and the other, as economic location, intangible and always changing, differing from person to person and within each according to their changing plans and subjective appreciations. Both terms have their place in our daily speech. But we must not confuse them. For the rest of this article, I'll use the word in its newer sense.

Creating Land

The obverse of location is *environment*, which is what gives any location such market value as it may have. Hence, land as economic location can be created, for better or for worse, by altering its environment.

Now, an owner who lets or sells anything at all to another naturally wants it to be serviceable for his customer so that his customer will be able to serve and continue serving him in exchange. More than that, if the owner is entrepreneurial, he looks for ways to improve whatever it is he has to offer. But if he has given his use to another, how can he do that? In the case of a site that he has let out to another, he can improve its location by tailoring its environment to his customer's needs. Thus a landowner who wants to improve the worth of a site he has leased out puts his attention not on the site itself, which is now under the control of another, but on its environment.

The shopping mall is a clear illustration. The owner customizes individual locations within the mall by a complex orchestration of the whole. He is alert to whatever on the mall might have environmental significance for the individually-leased sites. Beyond providing obvious environmental amenities such as adequate parking and attractive building and landscaping, he studies the placement of stores and common areas or facilities and their effect on each merchant's location. He strives for an optimal selection of types of merchants to create maximum draw from the market area collectively served by them. He wants, moreover, for every storekeeper to find himself a part of a vibrant community of merchants who together make an effective retailing team, each ready to cooperate in a hundred different ways such as participating in joint promotions, referring customers, maintaining a good appearance, keeping regular hours, or alerting one another promptly in security matters. Every team needs a coach, and the owner or mall manager is positioned to fill that role. He can provide effective leadership because the merchants recognize that he is not partisan, as each of them must be, but is concerned for the success of the mall as such. The presence of someone vitally interested in the whole and at once impartial is in itself a critical environmental feature, the catalyst helping all of this to happen—the owner striving to create optimal environment for each and every site within the mall.

Now, as the environment of each leased site continues ever outward, blind to property lines, so also does the mall owner's environmental concern extend beyond the bounds of the mall. He wants to promote those obvious things in the surrounding community that affect the merchants collectively, such as convenient freeways and other transportation to and from the market area they serve, making their sites more accessible. But more than that, he wants the surrounding host community itself to be affluent—since that means a prosperous customer base for his merchants. He realizes that the level of affluence in the host community is determined by many of the same things that give leased sites within the mall their utility, such as provision and maintenance of parks and well placed streets, water and power and other utilities, sewerage, security, and justice services, and many others. Consequently, he is concerned with the quality of management in the surrounding community just as within the mall itself, which is to say that he is interested in the quality of local government. He is concerned that municipal services be performed well and with the least tax burden on the residents, whether that means monitoring, informally supervising, subsidizing, or actually providing the services, alone or in collaboration with other landowners who might be similarly motivated. His nonpartisan interest in sound public administration extends, even though attenuated with increasing distance, beyond the host community to the county, state, nation, and even, in theory at least, the world.

Our example of the shopping mall has to do with an owner leasing to multiple tenants. A small landlord, renting or leasing to perhaps one tenant, has little hope of improving or rearranging the environment of that small parcel to make it more valuable to the tenant. He is almost as helpless as an individual owner who uses the land directly. He lets it for whatever use and level of use the existing surroundings permit and has little control over how community infrastructure is provided. If he looks for any improvement at all, it is for municipal government to intervene on his behalf. But as he enlarges his holding or combines with others to achieve a holding of more practical size, and acquires multiple tenants, perhaps cooperating with similarly motivated others in a realty association, he gains leverage over the environment. He finds first of all that in the very act of leasing to multiple tenants, each becomes a factor in the environment of every other, with excellent opportunity for synergy. By tenant selection, therefore, he strives to optimize his tenant mix. As his customer base increases, it becomes economically attractive for him to make still other and more substantial investments of an environmental nature. In so doing, he is creating land in the sense of that word as economic location.

Capital

Spencer Heath's thinking about capital builds on that of property as described above. The convention or covenant of ownership provides the static, *structural* precondition for human society—the mutually covenanted fences, the limits, the socially acknowledged jurisdictions or domains wherein each can make decisions and take action with full confidence that he will not be challenged. But such a covenant only provides social structure which, in itself, is static. It is the precondition of but does not constitute the dynamic *functioning* of human society, which consists in people voluntarily exchanging with one another, each serving many others and by many others being served, materially and spiritually. Society, as Heath used and operationalized the term, is more than a collection of people. It has to do with people behaving in a characteristic way. Society is that fraction of a population engaged in voluntary exchange[83]—and it is worthy of note that, as such, its boundaries are permeable.

Hence we often speak not of property alone, but bracket property and *contract,* ownership and exchange, structure and function. The covenant of ownership, or quiet possession, while useful by itself at the earliest levels of society where there is little exchange, makes *contract* possible, the drawing together (Latin *contrahere*), or, in English common-law parlance, a "meeting of minds," where people transcend the merely static covenant of ownership, agreeing on how they shall serve one another in the specific ways each wants to be served. It is a creative relationship in which wealth is produced simply through the purely psychological, the spiritual, act of first agreeing to exchange and then exchanging, not goods and services, but social authority, title, or *ownership* over goods and services.

So what does this have to do with capital? Exchange—serving others—is the tie-in. Capital is commonly thought of as tools—anything used to create wealth, including other tools. But this idea alone lacks social context; by this definition, Crusoe on his island employed capital. Spencer Heath, on the other hand, asks how, in a social context, wealth is created and concludes that it is by individuals specializing and serving others in ways that induce a voluntary return. As a concept appropriate to the social sciences, therefore, *capital,* as contrasted with consumer goods, consists of property that is being administered in a certain way; it is property that is being employed not directly for one's own benefit, but in serving others. He gives an example. A tobacconist has a selection of cigars in glass humidors displayed for sale. They are capital because they are being offered to others.

He decides to have one himself, selects one and puts it in his vest pocket to smoke on his lunch break. That cigar which he selected is no longer capital; now it is a consumer good. Before the tobacconist goes to lunch, however, he decides he won't have a cigar after all. He takes it from his vest pocket, puts it back into the humidor. Now it is capital again. Like Heath's treatment of "property," this is an operational definition. It is easy to apply a simple observational test. Capital may be administered in the service of others directly, as in the case of a retail inventory, or indirectly as in the case of a factory, the machine tools it houses, and the raw materials worked upon.

Thus we have from Spencer Heath a somewhat new way of looking at both *property* and *capital*. It is new in the sense of being descriptive of observed behavior rather than speculative about normative rights, and it is new also in taking explicitly into account the social context of the behavior and its functioning therein. Now, what does such a vantage prepare us to learn about the progress of civilization as a whole and, almost incidentally, the role that property in land may yet play in the ongoing drama of societal evolution?

III. The Progression of Civilization

The progress of civilization may be gauged by the degree to which property is administered as capital—the extent to which it is administered in the service of others and only indirectly for the benefit of the owner. Where exchange is little developed, people have few options but to fend for themselves, providing for themselves and their nearest kin and hoping to have enough. Not only is property scarce under such conditions, but very little of what exists is capital. As exchange becomes general, however, and people specialize and are more and more occupied in serving others and being served in turn, property not only becomes more abundant, it increasingly takes the form of capital. Out of the growing abundance of wealth that ensues, technology and aesthetic arts flourish and people exercise more choice over their lives, enhancing alike the quality of their individual lives and of their physical and social environment. The enriched social environment in turn affords still broader scope for the creative exercise of choice, and there is no apparent end to the process.

Land as Productive Capital

Now trace this progression in the case of a particular kind of property, namely, land. Along with every other kind of property, land also is increasingly being administered for the use of others. Whenever it is leased to others or is the site of any productive business enterprise, it is being administered as productive capital.[84] But one evolving use of land stands out from others, unique in its importance and promise. When it is let to more than one tenant, so that we have a multi-tenant property, it begins to take on the character of a community and, as such, has special needs. Questions arise how to provide and apportion the cost of amenities that must be enjoyed in common, such as protection, streets and other access ways, and how to augment or diminish neighborhood effects that come into play from differing land uses.

We must have services to accommodate these collective needs. Such services will differ from private goods and services in the market that pertain to individuals and can be enjoyed wherever individuals may be. These common or community services, sometimes called public services, pertain not to individuals but to a *place*. To enjoy them an individual must go to the place where they are provided.

A formula for serving the collective needs of community living is probably as old as settled human society. An individual by the consensus of custom provides leadership and, among other things, parcels out unused land and receives value in exchange for his distributive function, the value received for this service coming out of the resulting productivity on the site. That productivity would have been impossible but for the secure tenure, the "quiet"—i.e. uncontested—possession that can only be realized through an allocation that is not arbitrary or by force but is carried out peaceably through the consensus of ownership.

This pattern obtains in many kinship societies, in which exchange occurs through the idiom of the gift and in which the elder is not an owner but a trustee, with the community members being beneficiary owners. The pattern obtains also in manorial societies, where kinship bonding gives way to incipient contractual arrangements. It obtains in modern urban society wherever we have a multiple-tenant property such as an inn or a hotel, an apartment building, an office building, a medical clinic, a science research center, a marina, a theme park, a shopping mall, a restaurant, a theater, a plane, a train, a ship at sea. With combinations of these and still other forms, the kinds and possibilities soar. In each, land is being owned and administered not for private consumption, to the exclusion of others, but as productive capital in the service of others as customers.[85]

Multi-tenant properties have had their greatest development since the end of World War II. Inspired by the insights of Spencer Heath some years ago, I identified multi-tenant properties as a class and sketched their history.[86] In their contemporary form in the United States they are a recent phenomenon, the oldest member of the group, the hotel, only dating back to the Tremont House which opened in Boston in 1829. The Tremont House was a dramatic departure from its country cousin, the old medieval inn, and is universally regarded as marking the beginning of the modern hotel industry. Apartment buildings also date from the nineteenth century, but less far back; the first to be built as such rather than being converted from a preexisting structure is said to have been completed in 1888 near Union Square, New York City. Office buildings, which caught the public imagination as "skyscrapers," date from about the same time.

But the dramatic growth and development of multi-tenant properties has come in the last fifty years. Many new forms have appeared since the Second World War, including marinas, manufactured-home (ground lease) communities, motels, medical clinics, shopping centers and malls, office and research parks, and complex mixed-use developments. At the close of World War II, less than a dozen shopping centers existed in the United States, none more than a small neighborhood convenience facility and all experimental. Even the name had yet to be coined. Today, in the United States alone, they number more than a hundred-thousand and range in size up to many millions of square feet of *leasable* space, not counting the extensive areas enjoyed in common such as accessways, parking fields and malls.[87] Much the same has occurred with hotels, some of which have grown in size and complexity to the point of being virtually self-contained cities. In terms of population, counting registered guests, service staff and daily visitors, these surpass in size the largest cities of the United States at the time of Independence—Philadelphia, New York, and Boston.

The dramatic growth in number, kind, size and complexity of these specialized community forms from the last decades of the

twentieth century is without precedent in human history. Yet
even today, the social sciences are virtually barren of literature
in this area. For many of the reasons mentioned earlier, property
in land tends to be ignored.

Are multi-tenant properties harbingers of a key evolutionary
advance?

The great significance of multi-tenant properties lies, of
course, in their resemblance to communities as we know them.
A hotel, for example, has many similarities to what comes to
mind for most people when they think of a community. It has
its private and common areas. Its corridors are its streets and
alleys, while the lobby, sometimes elaborately landscaped, is
the town square. It operates a security system and distributes
utilities. Generally it has shopping, dining, theater and other
entertainment facilities, and often professional offices, medical
services, and perhaps even a chapel. It has a transit system which,
as it happens, operates not horizontally but vertically.

For another illustration, consider the shopping mall. It has
the same general characteristics as the hotel, but with features
uniquely its own. Rather than catering to a predominantly
transient population, its clientele are established merchants
comprising a retailing team. As noted earlier, the manager, being
vitally interested in the success of the whole enterprise on which
his revenue from the land depends, and therefore non-partisan,
finds himself uniquely positioned to provide leadership.[88]
This new, entrepreneurial leadership, entirely foreign to the
experience of merchants on traditional "Main Street USA," has
become an underlying premise of mall retailing.

Thus the infrastructure and management needs of multi-
tenant properties closely parallel those of communities as we are
accustomed to think of them. What opens the mind to a world of

possibilities is the fact that all of these community needs are met, and with increasing sophistication, through wholly free-market processes.[89] None of the Byzantine panoply of politics—voting, taxation, burdensome regulation and licensing requirements, unresponsive bureaucracies, politically correct ideologies, inherent conflicts of interest on the part of the administrators, has any place in the operation of multi-tenant properties.[90]

Such properties are expressions of a new kind of competitive *business*, namely that of creating, developing, fostering, managing, marketing, maintaining and enhancing optimal human habitat. Not only have many new and specialized forms evolved, serving new economic niches, but the trend has been for these specialized forms to combine, much as atoms of different kinds combine to form complex molecules. By so doing, they are fulfilling a demand for less specialized, ever more *generalized* habitats.

Here is a tantalizing question. At some point, might it not occur to developers of these properties that it would be but a small jump for their industry to develop and operate entire towns and cities on a leasehold basis?

One major step has yet to be achieved in the prototypical developments described here. That step is to generate their utilities on-site—ideally as an environmentally-friendly, managed-energy system with zero discharge. This will enable them not only to vastly increase their services to their residents, but at the same time to escape the political grid. Freedom from the bureaucratic umbilical will enable community development to take place anywhere in the world, on land or sea. Alvin Lowi shows how technology already developed makes this economically feasible.[91] Should such wholly contractual towns and cities come into being, they will offer conventional bureaucratic, taxation-dependent communities the first competition the world has known.

Conclusion

Locke's labor theory of ownership served the rising middle class in its struggle against the monarch and his tax collectors, but did posterity an enormous disservice. Adopted uncritically by Karl Marx, Henry George and others and used to attack and discredit the institution of property in land, it has led to no end of tragedy and mischief in the world. If, for lack of understanding, property in land continues undefended from government encroachment, far worse could lie ahead.

The formula of homesteading or mixing one's labor with land is still the basis of the normative, or moralizing, approach of classical liberals in thinking about property. A more scientific, descriptive manner of inquiry could lead to a reassessment of property in land as the creative social institution it is, enabling us to see and strongly assert the importance of the historic separation of land and state. Let us recognize the service that owners of land, like the owners of any other kind of property, perform in distributing "quiet possession." For if it were not for *owners*, access to sites and resources would be precarious or nonexistent. Let us acknowledge then the creativity and vast potential of property in land administered as capital in the service of others. Already the ugly duckling, private property in land, is showing white feathers—on its way, perhaps, to becoming freedom's white swan.

Major Works of Spencer Heath MacCallum

Print

Alvin Lowi Jr., and Spencer Heath MacCallum, "Community Technology: Liberating Community Development," January 10, 2021.

E. C. Riegel, *Flight from Inflation: The Monetary Alternative* ed. Spencer Heath MacCallum and George Morton (Los Angeles: Heather Foundation, 1978), https://reinventingmoney.files.wordpress.com/2015/05/flight.pdf.

E. C. Riegel, *The New Approach to Freedom, Together with Essays on the Separation of Money and State*, ed. Spencer Heath MacCallum and George Morton (Los Angeles: Heather Foundation, 1976). http://www.newapproachtofreedom.info/documents/naf.pdf. (This book was printed privately by its author in 1949, under the name of the Valun Institute for Monetary Research.)

Michael van Notten, *The Law of the Somalis: A Stable Foundation for Economic Development in the Horn of Africa*, ed. Spencer Heath MacCallum (Trenton, NJ: Red Sea Press, 2005), https://www.amazon.com/Law-Somalis-Foundation-Economic-Development/dp/156902250X.

Spencer H. MacCallum *The Art of Community,* Institute for Humane Studies, Arlington, VA, 1970. https://archive.org/details/artofcommunity00maccguat.

Spencer H. MacCallum, "A Model Lease for ORBIS," *Voluntaryist* 81 (August 1996), http://voluntaryist.com/backissues/081.pdf.

Spencer H. MacCallum, "A Short Perspective on Land and Social Evolution," *Voluntaryist*, http://voluntaryist.com/articles/issue-139/short-perspective-land-social-evolution/.

Spencer H. MacCallum, "Associated Individualism: A Victorian Dream of Freedom," *Reason*, April 1972, 17–24, https://www.unz.com/print/Reason-1972apr-00017/.

Spencer H. MacCallum, "E. C. Riegel on Money," The Heather Foundation, Los Angeles, CA, January 2008, http://www.newapproachtofreedom.info/documents/AboutRiegel.pdf.

Spencer H. McCallum, "Freedom's Ugly Duckling: A Fresh Take on Private Property in Land," archived on the website of the Explorers Foundation, accessed February 19, 2021, https://www.explorersfoundation.org/archive/maccallum-duckling.pdf. (Reproduced here.) An earlier version is: Spencer H. MacCallum, "Freedom's Ugly Duckling: A Fresh Take on Private Property in Land," *Libertarian Papers* 7, no. 2 (2015), http://libertarianpapers.org/wp-content/uploads/2015/10/article/2015/10/lp-7-2-33.pdf.

Spencer H. MacCallum, "In Search of a Word: Limited Government versus 'Anarchy,'" *Voluntaryist*, no. 82, October, 1996, http://voluntaryist.com/articles/issue-82/search-word-limited-government-versus-anarchy/.

Spencer H. MacCallum, "Residential Politics: How Democracy Erodes Community," *Critical Review* 17, nos. 3–4 (2006), https://www.tandfonline.com/doi/abs/10.1080/08913810508443646.

Spencer H. MacCallum, "The Legacy of E. C. Riegel," Beyond Money, September 7, 2009, https://beyondmoney.net/tag/maccallum/.

Spencer H. MacCallum, "The Quickening of Social Evolution: Perspectives on Proprietary (Entrepreneurial) Communities," *Independent Review* 2, no. 2 (Fall 1997): 287–302, https://www. independent.org/pdf/tir/tir_02_2_maccallum.pdf.

Spencer Heath MacCallum and Alvin Lowi, "A Summary of the Philosophy of Spencer Heath," *Libertarian Papers* 10, no. 1 (2018), http://libertarianpapers.org/wp-content/ uploads/2018/08/post/2018/08/lp-10-1-6.pdf.

Spencer Heath MacCallum and Joyce Brand, *Economics and the Spiritual Life of Free Men: Re-Imagining Our Emergent World Society* (The Science of Society Foundation, 2020).

Spencer Heath MacCallum, "A Peaceful Ferment in Somalia," Independent Institute, Oakland, CA, June, 1998, https://www. independent.org/publications/article.asp?id=126.

Spencer Heath MacCallum, "A Skeptic's View of One's *Right* to Defensive Force," *Voluntaryist*, no. 169 (2nd Quarter 2016), http://voluntaryist.com/backissues/169.pdf.

Spencer Heath MacCallum, "Introduction: Chronology and Perspective on the Mata Ortiz Phenomenon," *KIVA: Journal of Southwestern Anthropology and History* 60, no. 1 (1994), https:// doi.org/10.1080/00231940.1994.11758256.

Spencer Heath MacCallum, "Looking Back and Forward," *Voluntaryist*, 2003, http://voluntaryist.com/how-i-became-a-voluntaryist/looking-back-and-forward-by-spencer-heath-maccallum/.

Spencer Heath MacCallum, "Pioneering an Art Movement in Northern Mexico: The Potters of Mata Ortiz," *KIVA: Journal of Southwestern Anthropology and History* 60, no. 1 (1994), https:// doi.org/10.1080/00231940.1994.11758259.

Spencer Heath MacCallum, "Politics versus Proprietorship: Remarks Prefatory to Discussion of the *Orbis* Constitution for Proprietary Communities," Free Nation Foundation, 1996, http://freenation.org/a/f34m1.html.

Spencer Heath MacCallum, "The Enterprise of Community: Social and Environmental Implications of Administering Land as Productive Capital," *Journal of Libertarian Studies* 17, no. 4 (Fall 2003). Revised by the author 2007, https://explorersfoundation.org/archive/280t1-maccallum-ec.pdf.

Spencer Heath MacCallum, "The Entrepreneurial Community in Light of Advancing Business Practices and Technologies," chapter 12 in *The Half-Life of Policy Rationales: How New Technology Affects Old Policy Issues*, ed. Fred E. Foldvary and Daniel B. Klein (New York: New York University Press, 2003), https://www.amazon.com/Half-Life-Policy-Rationales-Technology-Institute/dp/0814747779.

Spencer Heath MacCallum, "The Rule of Law without the State," *Mises Daily*, September 12, 2007, https://mises.org/library/rule-law-without-state.

Spencer Heath MacCallum, "Werner K. Stiefel's Pursuit of a Practicum of Freedom," *Voluntaryist*, 2006, http://voluntaryist.com/forthcoming/stiefel.html.

Spencer Mac Callum, "The Social Nature of Ownership," *Modern Age* (Winter 1964–65). Posted at Intercollegiate Studies Institute, https://isi.org/wp-content/uploads/2014/10/maccallum.pdf?x66229.

Spencer MacCallum, "From Upstate New York to the Horn of Africa," *Liberty Magazine*, May 2005.

Videos

Spencer MacCallum "Creation of Entrepreneurial Communities," NewMedia UFM (Universidad Francisco Marroquín), Guatemala, July 31, 2013, YouTube video, https://www.youtube.com/watch?v=hLSbAOo_E8A.

Spencer MacCallum, "Enterprise of Community," NewMedia UFM (Universidad Francisco Marroquín), Guatemala, August 1, 2013, YouTube video, https://www.youtube.com/watch?v=KUNQG5Akqlw.

Spencer MacCallum, "Property: A Social Approach," NewMedia UFM (Universidad Francisco Marroquín), Guatemala, July 31,2013, YouTube video, https://www.youtube.com/watch?v=w8E-wP9kFPw.

Spencer MacCallum, "Spencer Heath and a Libertarian Tradition," NewMedia UFM (Universidad Francisco Marroquín), Guatemala, July 30,2013, https://newmedia.ufm.edu/video/spencer-heath-and-a-libertarian-tradition/.

V-50 Panel Discussion, "Private Cities," at Libertopia, October 17, 2010, with Spencer MacCallum, Jay Snelson, Peter Bos, Alvin Lowi, and Chas Holloway, YouTube video, https://www.youtube.com/watch?v=w6gu7-svjnU.

Major Works of Spencer Heath

Alvin Lowi Jr., "The Legacy of Spencer Heath: A Former Student Remembers the Man and Offers Some Observations on the Scientific Orientation of His Work," http://www.logan.com/afi/spencer1.html, http://www.logan.com/afi/spencer2.html, http://www.logan.com/afi/spencer3.html.

Spencer Heath, *Citadel, Market and Altar: Emerging Society, Outline of Socionomy, Emerging Society*, Baltimore: Science of Society Foundation, 1957.

Spencer Heath, *The Inspiration of Beauty, Human Emergence into the Divine by Creative Artistry*, 16-page pamphlet, August 1960.

Spencer Heath, *Private Property in Land Explained: Some New Light on the Social Order and Its Mode of Operation*, 22-page pamphlet (New York: The Freeman, 1939).

Spencer Heath, *Progress & Poverty Reviewed & Its Fallacies Exposed*, 23-page pamphlet with supplementary material (New York: The Freeman, 1952).

Spencer Heath, *Real Estate: How to Raise and Restore Its Income and Value. Questions for the Consideration of Land Owners*, Elkridge, MD, 1940.

Spencer Heath, *Politics versus Proprietorship: A Fragmentary Study of Social and Economic Phenomena with Particular Reference to the Public Administrative Functions Belonging to Proprietorship as a Creative Social Agency*, 71-page pamphlet (New York: The Freeman, 1936).

Appendix
Operation Atlantis

Businessman Werner Stiefel launched Operation Atlantis in 1968. His goal was to create a sovereign nation in international waters beyond the reach of other nation-states. Inspired by the works of Ayn Rand, Stiefel wrote his own book *The Story of Operation Atlantis* as a call to action for libertarians, a call he himself answered with his time, money, and intellect.

He brought together a group of like-minded libertarians at the Sawyerkill Motel in Saugerties, New York. The location was close to one of his plants. Stiefel was head of Stiefel Laboratories, which by 2006 was the largest privately owned dermatological company in the world.

Operation Atlantis launched a thirty-eight-foot ferro-cement boat in 1971, which was piloted to a spot in the Bahamas. Shortly thereafter the boat was sunk by a hurricane. Stiefel bought a second boat and headed to Tortuga Island near the northwest coast of Hispaniola, but the Haitian government drove them off. The Haitian navy also drove them away when they tried dredging sand for a new island at nearby Silver Shoals Cay. Stiefel made a few more attempts to build or buy what became known as a seastead, without success.

In a tribute to Stiefel written upon his death in 2006, Spencer MacCallum recalled their interactions:

> Around 1970, I made the acquaintance of Werner, who was developing plans to build a free community. While the community would need to be effectively governed, it would

differ from communities as we know them by being internally
consistent. In no way would its management infringe
upon property rights. There would be no taxation or other
discretionary authority over anyone's person or property.[92]

While discussing the project at a coffee shop near Spencer's
home in San Pedro, California, Spencer made the connection
between Operation Atlantis and the proprietary communities
he had been studying. Werner immediately saw the benefits.

Werner saw that the master-lease form would be critical to
the success of Atlantis. It would be Atlantis' social software,
as it were, capable of generating an elaborate but internally
consistent web of relationships, all spelled out in the wording
of the leases, subleases, sub-subleases, etc. The sum of the
agreements in effect at any given point in time would be the
written constitution of Atlantis. They could be as specialized
and distinct as circumstances might warrant, so long as they
did not contradict any part of the master-lease form.

Without a body of legislated rules to fall back upon, the
master-lease form would have to provide for every conceivable
contingency. Werner gave me the task of drafting it. It was a
moment of truth. But I couldn't dodge the assignment, since
I had studied the question from the broad viewpoint of social
anthropology and had published the first description of
multi-tenant income properties as a distinct class of social
phenomena (*The Art of Community*, Institute for Humane
Studies, 1970). No mere theoretician, Werner assigned me a 2%
equity in the venture.

Werner's master-lease form not only survived his Atlantis
project, it took on a life of its own. With Werner's approval,

it was published in several iterations, giving many people an opportunity to criticize it and offer improvements. But because Werner was leery of prematurely drawing the attention of the world's governments to the idea of private settlement of the open seas, it carried no reference to Atlantis. It appeared as a purely heuristic exercise in the free-market provision of community services in a made-up setting called "Orbis," one of a hypothetical cluster of settlements in outer space.[93]

"A Model Lease for Orbis" in its entirety can be found at http://www.freenation.org/a/f33m1.html.

Sources

Isabelle Simpson. "Operation Atlantis: A Case-Study in Libertarian Island Micronationality," Montreal. McGill University, September 27, 2016, https://www.shimajournal.org/issues/v1on2/e.-Simpson-Shima-v1on2.pdf.

Preston Martin. "Project Atlantis: The First Libertarian Seastead." Startup Societies Foundation, June 4, 2007, https://www.startupsocieties.org/blog/project-atlantis-the-first-libertarian-seastead.

Spencer Heath MacCallum. "Werner K. Stiefel's Pursuit of a Practicum of Freedom," *Voluntaryist*, no. 134, http://voluntaryist.com/articles/issue-134/werner-k-stiefels-pursuit-practicum-freedom/.

——. "A Model Lease for Orbis," Free Nation Foundation, Spring 1996, http://www.freenation.org/a/f33m1.html.

——. "Politics versus Proprietorship: Remarks Prefatory to Discussion of the *Orbis* Constitution for Proprietary Communities," Free Nation Foundation, April 1996, http://freenation.org/a/f34m1.html.

Endnotes

Introduction

1. Spencer Heath MacCallum, *The Art of Community* (Menlo Park, CA: Institute for Humane Studies, 1970).

2. Alvin Lowi Jr., "Spencer Heath's Personal Trinity," Logan.com, accessed February 18, 2021, http://www.logan.com/afi/spencer2.html.

3. Calvin Duke, *Entrepreneurial Communities: An Alternative to the State* (Colorado Springs , CO: Book Villages, 2020), 16–17.

Chapter 2

4. Spencer Heath, *Citadel, Market and Altar: Emerging Society, Outline of Socionomy*, Science of Society Foundation: Baltimore, MD, 1957.

5. See David Gordon, "Murray N. Rothbard," LewRockwell.com, April 18, 2013, https://www.lewrockwell.com/2013/04/david-gordon/who-is-murray-rothbard/. Rothbard was closely associated with the Ludwig von Mises Institute from its founding in 1982 by Llewellyn H. Rockwell Jr. This organization became the main vehicle for the promotion of his ideas, and he served as its academic vice president. Gordon, "Murray N. Rothbard," Mises Institute website, Profiles, accessed February 12, 2021, https://mises.org/profile/murray-n-rothbard.

6. Robert Leeson, ed., *Hayek: A Collaborative Biography, Part IX: The Divine Right of the 'Free' Market* (Cham, Switzerland: Springer, 2017), 180.

7. Llewellyn H. Rockwell Jr., ed., *Murray N. Rothbard: In Memoriam* (Auburn, AL: Ludwig von Mises Institute, 1995), 117.

8. Charley Reese, "Why I Am Not a Libertarian," *Orlando Sentinel*, April 15, 2001, https://www.orlandosentinel.com/news/os-xpm-2001-04-15-0104140035-story.html.

9. Spencer Heath MacCallum, *Economics and the Spiritual Life of Free Men: Re-Imagining Our Emergent World Society* (n.p.: The Science of Society Foundation, 2018). This work is published under a Creative Commons Attribution 4.0 license. 415-429-6753 CC.

Chapter 3

10. Fred E. Foldvary, "Heath: Estranged Georgist," *American Journal of Economics and Sociology* 63, no. 2 (April 2004): 411, https://onlinelibrary.wiley.com/doi/10.1111/j.0002-9246.2004.00295.x.

11. Joseph Gilly, "The Art of Community," *Reason*, April 1972 (see intro., n. 1).

12. *Politics versus Proprietorship: A Fragmentary Study of Social and Economic Phenomena with Particular Reference to the Public Administrative Functions Belonging to Proprietorship as A Creative Social Agency* (71-page pamphlet), reprinted by the *Freeman*, 1936, ASIN: B0008C4IDU.

13. Alvin Lowi Jr., "The Legacy of Spencer Heath" (see intro., n. 2).

14. C. Lowell Harriss, "Rothbard's Anarcho-Capitalist Critique," 368n4, https://www.cooperative-individualism.org/andelson-robert_critics-of-henry-george-1979-25-rothbard-by-c-lowell-harriss.pdf.

15. Spencer Heath, *Citadel, Market and Altar* (see chap. 2, n. 1).

16. Published in the Autumn 1999 issue of *Formulations*, http://freenation.org/a/f71h5.html.

17. Science of Society Foundation website, accessed February 12, 2021, https://scienceofsociety.net/home-page/.

18. Spencer Heath MacCallum and Alvin Lowi, "A Summary of the Philosophy of Spencer Heath," *Libertarian Papers* 10, no. 1 (2018): 101–2, 100, http://libertarianpapers.org/wp-content/uploads/2018/08/post/2018/08/lp-10-1-6.pdf.

Chapter 4

19. Gilly, "The Art of Community" (see intro., no. 1).

20. Murray N. Rothbard, "Floyd Arthur 'Baldy' Harper, RIP," *Mises Daily Articles*, August 17, 2007, https://mises.org/library/floyd-arthur-baldy-harper-rip.

21. John Chamberlain, *The Roots of Capitalism* (Princeton, NJ: D. Van Nostrand, 1959), 92–93, 214–15.

22. Spencer Heath MacCallum, *The Art of Community* (Menlo Park, CA: Institute for Humane Studies, 1970).

23. Not to be confused with another organization with the same name started in 1976 whose goal was to educate America "in the twin pillars of liberty and responsibility so that we may preserve our freedoms." Free Enterprise Institute website, accessed February 15, 2021, https://thefreeenterpriseinstitute.org.

24. Fifty years later at the first Libertopia, Spencer gave a lecture on Entrecomms and led a panel that included people who attended his Free Enterprise Institute course in 1964.

25. Peter Bos, *The Road to Freedom and the Demise of Nations States,* (Lulu Publishing Services, 2018), (2018), https://www.amazon.com/Road-Freedom-Demise-Nation-States/dp/1483431444.

26. "Who We Are," Institute for Humane Studies website, accessed February 15, 2021, https://theihs.org/who-we-are/.

Chapter 5

27. Spencer Mac Callum, "The Social Nature of Ownership," *Modern Age* (Winter 1964–65), https://isi.org/wp-content/uploads/2014/10/maccallum.pdf?x66229.

28. E. C. Riegel, *The New Approach to Freedom: Together with Essays on the Separation of Money and State*, ed. Spencer Heath MacCallum and George Morton (Los Angeles: Heather Foundation, 1976), http://www.newapproachtofreedom.info/documents/naf.pdf.

29. E. C. Riegel, *Flight from Inflation: The Monetary Alternative*, ed. Spencer Heath MacCallum and George Morton (Los Angeles: Heather Foundation, 1978).

30. Alvin Lowi Jr. and Spencer Heath MacCallum, "Community Technology: Liberating Community Development," January 10, 2021. This paper was originally drafted in 2013.

31. Spencer Heath MacCallum, "Werner K. Stiefel's Pursuit of a Practicum of Freedom," *Voluntaryist*, accessed February 15, 2021, http://voluntaryist.com/forthcoming/stiefel.html.

32. Spencer H. MacCallum, "A Model Lease for ORBIS," *Voluntarist* 81 (August, 1996), http://voluntaryist.com/backissues/081.pdf.

33. See chap. 5, n. 4. Spencer Heath MacCallum, *The Art of Community.*

34. Gilly, "The Art of Community" (see intro., no. 1).

Chapter 6

35. Kiara Maureen Hughes, "The Women Potters of Mata Ortiz: Growing Empowerment through Artistic Work," University of New Mexico UNM Digital Repository, July 1, 2009, https://digitalrepository.unm.edu/cgi/viewcontent.cgi?article=1033&context=anth_etds.

36. Hughes, "Women Potters."

Chapter 7

37. Richard O. Hammer, "Toward a Free Nation," 1993, http://freenation.org/toward.html.

38. "TCSR Research Division," accessed February 15, 2021, http://www.logan.com/afi/lowi.html.

39. See chapter 12 in Fred E. Foldvary and Daniel B. Klein, eds., *The Half-Life of Policy Rationales: How New Technology Affects Old Policy Issues* (New York: University Press, 2003).

40. Bruce Canter, comments made in an email to the author, February 7, 2021.

41. Spencer H. MacCallum, "The Enterprise of Community: Market Competition, Land, and Environment," *Journal of Libertarian Studies* 17, no. 4 (Fall 2003), 1–15, https://mises.org/library/enterprise-community-market-competition-land-and-environment.

42. Michael van Notten, *The Law of the Somalis: A Stable Foundation for Economic Development in the Horn of Africa*, ed. Spencer Heath MacCallum (Trenton, NJ: Red Sea Press, 2005).

Chapter 8

43. Spencer Heath MacCallum, "Pioneering an Art Movement in Northern Mexico: The Potters of Mata Ortiz," *Kiva: Journal of Southwestern Anthropology and History* 60, no. 1 (Fall, 1994), 71–91, https://doi.org/10.1080/00231940.1994.11758259.

44. Hughes, "Women Potters".

45. Hughes, "Women Potters," 172.

46. IMBd, "The Renaissance of Mata Ortiz (2010)," IMDb.com, accessed February 15, 2021, https://www.imdb.com/title/tt1729570/?ref_=nm_knf_t2.

47. Hughes, "Women Potters" 259.

48. Walter P. Parks, *The Miracle of Mata Ortiz: Juan Quezada and the Potters of Northern Chihuahua* (Tucson: Rio Nuevo, 2011).

49. Walter P. Parks, in an email to the author, February 3, 2021.

50. Suzanne Muchnic, "All from the Clay of Mata Ortiz," *Los Angeles Times*, June 29, 2007, https://www.latimes.com/archives/la-xpm-2007-jun-29-et-ceramics29-story.html.

51. Walter Parks and Richard O'Connor, "A Great Loss," Mata Ortiz Calendar Online, posted January 1, 2021, http://mataortizcalendar.net/editorial.html.

52. James Blake Wiener, "Casas Grandes," *Ancient History Encyclopedia*, https://www.ancient.eu/Casas_Grandes/.

Chapter 9

53. Zachary Caceres, "Spencer MacCallum & The World He Made: A Eulogy (1931-2020)," https://www.notion.so/Spencer-MacCallum-The-World-He-Made-A-Eulogy-1931-2020-10e1026cae664b7685e1c37c7c283e69. See also Zach Caceres (https://www.zach.dev). Reproduced with permission.

Chapter 11

54. The lesser-known first edition, which I prefer, was published in 1898 under the title *Tomorrow: A Peaceful Path to Real Reform*.

Chapter 12

55. For an early history of the multi-tenant income property, *The Art of Community*. Menlo Park, CA: Institute for Humane Studies, (1970, 7–48).

56. Boston Public Library, Reference. Boston had 15,520 inhabitants in 1765. By the time of the United States Census of 1790, this had grown to 18,038—freemen only. Counting room guests, service staff, and visitors, the population of the MGM Grand ranges between 35,000 and 70,000 persons daily (MGM Grand public relations department 1998).

57. Automotive retail trade includes dealers and service stations.

58. For speculation on the reasons for this and some of its attendant complications, see MacCallum, "Residential politics: How democracy erodes community," Critical Review Vol. 17 Nos. 3-4 (Fall/Winter 2005).

59. "Is not the residents' association, with compulsory membership, compulsory dues, and democratic voting rules, simply a local government under a different name?" For a discussion of homeowners' associations, see MacCallum (forthcoming in *Critical Review*).

60. For a detailed historical account, see Evan McKenzie (1994). Evan McKenzie. *Privatopia: Homeowner Associations and the Rise of Residential Private Government* (Yale University Press, 1994).

61. My grandfather, Spencer Heath (1876–1963), was an engineer, lawyer, poet, philosopher of science, and social philosopher, as well as a pioneer in early aviation, developing the first machine mass production of airplane propellers in 1912 and ten years later demonstrating at Boling Field the first engine powered and controlled variable and reversible pitch propeller. Heath was awakened to social issues as a young man by the widely influential novel *Looking Backward*, in which author Edward Bellamy set forth compellingly his socialist vision of the future. Rejecting that after six months and looking for something more workable, Heath found himself attracted to Henry George's emphasis on free trade. This began a thirty-five-year active involvement in the Georgist movement, which focused his attention on land. Studying George's proposal that government collect and disburse all land rents, Heath came to a recognition of the importance of the private administration of land as productive capital. This new perspective he outlined in 1936 in a self-published monograph, *Politics versus Proprietorship*, and elaborated in 1957 in his main work on society, *Citadel, Market and Altar*. Heath's published and unpublished writings are administered by the Heather Foundation, 713 W. Spruce #48, Deming, NM 88030. sm@look.net.

Chapter 13

62. Murray Rothbard in 1957 wrote, "most present-day economists ignore the land question and Henry George altogether ... Yet there is a land question, and ignoring it does not lay the matter to rest." Cf. Murray N. Rothbard, "The Single Tax: Economic and Moral Implications," *Mises Daily*, December 6, 2011. Much of the discussion of land in the twentieth century is covered in Robert V. Andelson (ed.), *Critics of Henry George: An Appraisal of their Strictures on Progress and Poverty*, Vd.2. Oxford: Wiley-Blackwell, 2004.

63. Spencer Heath, *Citadel, Market and Altar: Emerging Society*. Baltimore: Science of Society Foundation, 1957, pp. 95, 106, 238.

64. John Locke, *Second Treatise of Government: An Essay Concerning the True Original, Extent and End of Civil Government*. Enhanced Media, [1690] 2014.

65. Karl Marx and Frederick Engels, *Manifesto of the Communist Party*. Marxist Internet Archive, [1848] 2010.

66. An address given in Metropolitan Hall, San Francisco, February 4, 1890, available from the Robert Schalkenbach Foundation, New York City. Harold Kyriazi notes that while George stopped short of advocating

complete abolition of private property in land, proposing instead that landowners keep title and a very small, nominal fraction of the rent, it was not because he thought landowners provided a modicum of service but unequivocally because he believed his reform "could be enacted more smoothly if it maintained the appearance of continued full private ownership of land." Cf Harold Kyriazi, "Reckoning with Rothbard," in Robert V. Andelson (ed.), *Critics of Henry George: An appraisal of their strictures on Progress and Poverty*, Chapter 31, Vol. 2, *The American Journal of Economics and Sociology*, Annual Supplement, Vol. 63 No.2, April 2004.

67. Although he felt he had not researched the question enough to write about it, F. A. Harper was of the opinion that, but for Henry George, Marxism might never have enjoyed much influence. Harper believed that Marx had given up his cause at the time of George's European speaking tours. The overwhelming success of those tours, however, brought a flood of new interest in and support for Marxism. (Personal communication) Murray Rothbard notes that according to E. R. Pease, socialist historian and longtime secretary of the Fabian Society, *Progress and Poverty* "beyond all question had more to do with the socialist revival of that period in England than any other book." Cf. Murray N. Rothbard, "The Single Tax: Economic and Moral Implications," *Mises Daily*, December 6, 2011.

68. The game of Monopoly, originally named "The Landlord's Game," was invented around the turn of the twentieth century by Georgists Elizabeth Magee Phillips and her sister (the Robert Schalkenbach Foundation, New York City, is currently supporting research on this history). The term "rent seeking" was originated by Anne Krueger in 1974. It was rapidly adopted, especially by the Public Choice school of economics, to denote the behavior of persons seeking government privilege. While I do not know Krueger's intent, my inference is that she considers the behavior of land-owners to be more political than free-market. Economist Fred Foldvary has proposed an alternative term, "transfer seeking" (personal communication April 23, 1997).

69. P. J. Hill, "Rerun: 'The Not So Wild West.'" *PERC Reports* 28 (2): 9, 2010.

70. Mark Brandly, "Including the Ocean Floor the Feds Own Much More Land Than You Think," *Mises Daily*, March 17, 2016. Areas affected are mapped. Due to research difficulties, however, not all government-controlled land, such as municipal, is counted.

71. For extended discussion, cf. Spencer MacCallum, "The Social Nature of Ownership." *Modern Age* 9 (1): 1964–1965.

73. Manuel F. Ayau, *Not a Zero-Sum Game: The Paradox of Exchange*. Guatemala City: Universidad Francisco Marroquín, 2007.

73. The writer was present when Harper and his family visited and inspected Roadsend Gardens March 24–26, 1957 (Spencer Heath Archive, Items 2529, 2531, 2540). Harper ultimately declined the offer, thinking that the intellectual climate in California at that time would be more hospitable for what he wanted to create.

74. Apart from Harper and Heath there has been in recent times little interest in developing a natural science of human organization. A notable exception was British social anthropologist A. R. Radcliffe-Brown, author of *A Natural Science of Society*, Glencoe, IL: The Free Press & The Falcon's Wing Press, 1957.

75. Harper wanted to create a space with an atmosphere that would be conducive to breakthrough thinking, a special kind of community of scholars. He dreamed of inviting a dozen or more retired but intellectually active seniors from all fields to take up work space at the institute, using its tax-free status to help with their work and enjoying as much privacy as they wished but free to mingle with others especially at lunch time, as had been the practice at FEE. Realizing that breakthroughs more often come from young people, he would invite young people as guests to freely enjoy the same facilities, thinking the opportunity of their rubbing elbows with seasoned older scholars would be the key part of the formula he strove for. This was his unique vision for promoting new understanding that would lead to human freedom. His untimely death prevented it from being realized. IHS today mentors graduate students, assists them in obtaining grants and academic positions, and teaches through seminars and symposia.

76. Percy W. Bridgman, *The Nature of Physical Theory*. Princeton University Press, 1936, Chapter 2, "Operations," pp. 5–15.

77. John R. Commons, *Institutional Economics*. New York: MacMillan, 1934, p. 169.

78. T. E. Cliffe Leslie, Introduction to Laveleye, Émile de. *Primitive property*. London: MacMillan, 1877.

79. Spencer Heath, *Citadel, Market and Altar: Emerging Society*. Baltimore: Science of Society Foundation, 1957, p. 235.

80. Alvin Lowi, "The Nature of Property in Society," unpublished manuscript, 200.

81. Spencer MacCallum, "A Short Perspective on Land and Social Evolution," *Voluntaryist* 139:2008.

82. For an insightful discussion, cf. Peter St. Onge, "The Fallacy of 'Buy Land— They're not making any More.'" *Mises Daily*, September 16, 2015.

83. Spencer Heath, *Citadel, Market and Altar: Emerging Society*. Baltimore: Science of Society Foundation, 1957, p. 231.

84. This statement would have been unacceptable to Henry George, for whom land was not and could not be capital as he used the term. His argument was that the land owner merely as such performs no service because he has expended no labor in making land. Therefore, when he rents or sells it, the benefit is all one way. No value is created, but rather value is drained from the land user, who thereby becomes the victim of legal monopoly, or privilege.

    The hidden error lies in thinking that it is the accumulated labor expended in making something that induces a voluntary recompense in exchange. In fact, what induces a voluntary recompense is an owner's transfer of ownership to another. His ownership is his title—which is to say his entitlement—to the thing in question, and it is this intangible that he conveys. Conveyance of the thing itself would only give a precarious possession; it would not give "quiet possession," where "quiet" means at old English Common Law "unchallenged." Quiet possession is obtainable only by a transfer of ownership.

    This service of transferring ownership, which none but an owner can perform, is not physical. It arises only at the point of conveyance by rental, sale, or gift, and is entirely social and psychological in its nature. The owner of land performs this service in the market exactly as does the owner of any other kind of property. It makes no difference whether the thing owned is tangible or intangible, natural or artifact.

    Thus the service an owner uniquely performs is his act of transferring ownership, his social authority, which is his and his alone to do. At other times he might be said to perform a standby service, but for this he receives no recompense; for value arises only at the point of exchange. When such value does arise, it, too, is intangible, consisting of a conveyance of ownership in return. All process of exchange in society, strictly speaking, is not physical, but social and psychological.

85. See especially Spencer MacCallum, "The Enterprise of Community: Social and Environmental Implications of Administering Land as Productive Capital." *Journal of Libertarian Studies* 17 (4): 1–15, 2003. Revised by the author.

86. Spencer MacCallum, *The Art of Community*. Menlo Park, CA: Institute for Humane Studies, 1970.

87. International Council of Shopping Centers (ICSC). "Shopping Center Facts and Stats," 2015.

88. Africanist anthropologist Paul Bohannan observed in private conversation with me that the role of the manager of a shopping center "is more than similar to . . . [in fact] it is precisely like that of the headman of an African village."

89. Two important early discussions of private, contractual provision of public community services are economist Raymond V. McNally, 1942, "Some Observations on the Nature of Public Enterprise," *Libertarian Papers* 6 (1) (2014), and Spencer Heath, "The Capitalist System," 1934, *Libertarian Papers* 7 (2) (2015). A later discussion is in Heath, *Citadel, Market and Altar*. Baltimore: Science of Society Foundation, 1957.

90. To avoid a common confusion, I must inject parenthetically that this remarkable class of property does not include condominiums, planned unit developments, or other forms of land *subdivision*. These represent consumer uses of land—owners getting together collectively to serve themselves rather than customers—and as such are not part of the trend toward land being administered as productive capital. They lack a concentrated entrepreneurial interest in the success of the development. Indeed, for a multi-tenant venture to subdivide and sell off its land—its productive capital—would be to put itself out of business.

91. Alvin Lowi and Spencer MacCallum, "Community Technology: Liberating Community Development," Chapter 6 in Stefano Moroni and David Andersson (eds.), *Cities and Private Planning*. London: Edward Elgar, 2014.

Appendix

92. Spencer MacCallum, "Werner K. Stiefel's Pursuit of a Practicum of Freedom," LewRockwell.com, June 19, 2006, https://www.lewrockwell.com/2006/06/spencer-heath-maccallum/werner-k-stiefels-pursuit-of-a-practicumoffreedom.

93. MacCallum.

Mike Hamel is a storyteller by trade and the author/editor of more than 30 books on topics as wide-ranging as business, finance, political theory, healthcare, nonprofits, theology and children's books.

Learn more on Amazon,
https://www.amazon.com/Mike-Hamel/e/B001JSB7FE/
and Wikipedia, **https://en.wikipedia.org/wiki/Mike_Hamel**.
You can contact Mike at **emtcom@comcast.net**.

Made in the USA
Columbia, SC
30 March 2021